W9-CED-704

Grace in the Wilderness

Books by **ARANKA SIEGAL**

Upon the Head of the Goat

A Childhood in Hungary 1939–1944

Grace in the Wilderness

After the Liberation 1945–1948

ARANKA SIEGAL

Grace in the Wilderness

AFTER THE LIBERATION
1945–1948

A SUNBURST BOOK
FARRAR, STRAUS AND GIROUX

Distributed in Canada by Douglas & McIntyre Ltd.
Printed in the United States of America
First edition, 1985
Sunburst edition, 2003
1 3 5 7 9 10 8 6 4 2

Library of Congress Cataloging-in-Publication Data
Siegal, Aranka.
Grace in the Wilderness.
1. Siegal, Aranka—Juvenile literature. 2. Holocaust survivors—Sweden—Biography—Juvenile literature. 3. Jews—Sweden—Biography—Juvenile literature. [1. Siegal, Aranka. 2. Holocaust survivors. 3. Jews—Sweden—Biography.] I. Title.

ISBN 0-374-42794-1 (pbk.)
DS135.S89S547 1985 85-20415

My thanks to my husband, Gilbert, and my
children, Risë and Joseph, for their untiring
support and encouragement

To the generous Swedish people,
who opened their hearts and their doors to us,
and to my brother-in-law Rulle,
who was one of them

Thus saith the Lord: "The people that were left of the sword have found grace in the wilderness . . ."

JEREMIAH 31

FROM LEFT TO RIGHT:
Two fellow survivors, Piri (Aranka Siegal) and Iboya

Grace in the Wilderness

I was afraid to step out into the dark and quiet area between the two barracks. The beams from yellow lights on high poles lit up the electrified wire fence surrounding the vast camp. Not a creature or shadow stirred. My awareness of the guards in their lookout towers was more mental than visual. That image had been fixed in my mind from my first sight of them months ago. Each tower had an SS uniformed guard and a machine gun, both at the ready to kill.

We had lost track of time. I could not even guess how many hours we had spent in conversation with Misha, the blockova in charge of barrack number 12. "Don't linger—make a dash for it," Misha warned as she held the door open for us.

My sister Iboya took my hand and we ran the twenty feet of bare ground. Holding our breath, we removed our wooden shoes and crept into our barrack, afraid of being discovered and punished by Vera, our own blockova. The large room was filled with so many women collapsed in sleep that Iboya and I had to be careful not to step on anyone. We were looking for our friends, the three Hollanders, to share our latest news. Ever since Christianstadt, our former concentration camp, we had lined up with them, five abreast. But the night had blackened the small windows and slits between the wall planks, making it impossible to pick them out from all the other prisoners with shorn heads. Moaning, grunting, and snoring merged into one sound. I stepped on a limp hand. Startled, the woman screamed out, "Two whores returning from prowling."

The truth was, we had been invited for tea. Given our circumstances, this was less believable than the woman's accusation; ordinary prisoners were not asked to tea by blockovas in Bergen-Belsen. Blockovas, in spite of their being Jewish inmates like the rest of us, treated us like slaves.

Misha had spotted Iboya talking to the Wehrmacht soldier during our evening roll call. As soon as the soldier had walked away, she came running over to us with a forced smile. She whispered to Iboya, "I like you. After the others go in, sneak over and come into my quarters. I'll make you some tea."

Stunned by the invitation, Iboya managed to answer, "This is my sister; can she come, too?"

"*Ja, ja*, that will be all right. Bring her."

Misha's room was at the end of her barrack. It was the size of a walk-in closet with a window opposite the entrance. A narrow bunk bed took up the left wall. Against the right wall stood a square table with a stool on either side. Next to it a small cupboard held some dishes and food. Misha had lit an alcohol stove on the table, and a white enamel pot was set on the blue flames. While the water simmered, she brought forth from the cupboard a whole loaf of bread and a block of cheese. I had not seen such an extravagance of food in one place since we left Christianstadt, where I had worked in the kitchen.

"Now I want to hear every word that soldier told you," Misha ordered, pushing Iboya toward one of the stools and seating herself on the other, hunched over and waiting. I stood close by Iboya's side and listened.

"About a week ago we were in line for roll call, like this evening, when he came over to me and asked us where we were from. He spoke in German. 'Hungary,' I answered him hesitantly. He said he was looking for a woman from Kosice, and her name was Sari Roth. I told him I didn't know her. He said, 'Ask around and I'll come by tomorrow.' He seemed sincere, but I did not trust him. Why would a German soldier, even if he was not an SS man, be interested in a Jewish woman, I wondered. The next time he came I lied and told him, 'I asked and looked for her, but had no luck. Nobody has heard of her.' Then he started talking to me in Hungarian. He said his troop was sent to Germany from Kosice and given German uniforms. And that Sari was his girlfriend. He also told me that the Germans were losing the war."

Iboya paused, her voice breathless, her eyes anxiously questioning Misha, as if to say, "Do you believe it?" Misha only urged Iboya, "Continue!"

"When he showed up today and asked me again if I had any news about Sari, I shook my head no. I could tell that he felt I still did not trust him. He motioned for me to follow him to the back of our barrack. There he first looked around to make sure nobody could see us. Squatting down, he drew a map in the dust with his stick. When he straightened up his face was wet and his shirt collar was stained with sweat. He carefully explained the lines he had drawn, showing the position of the Germans and the English at the front. Then he calculated the distance from the border to the camp and ended by saying, 'I hope you understand that I'm telling you this camp may be liberated within the next twenty-four hours.' "

Misha handed Iboya a pencil and paper. "Draw the map and try to remember everything exactly as he showed you."

I did not attempt to follow the drawing or their speculations but sat down cautiously on the edge of Misha's bed. It was all too incredible, watching Iboya with her shoulders pulled up, looking very important, the two of us inside a blockova's partition eating and drinking with her, like friends. The loaf of bread on the table was the equivalent of ten days' rations and the cheese unimaginable. The tea was bitter but hot, warming my empty and dehydrated stomach. Afraid the bread would be snatched away from me, I wanted to gulp down my thick slice spread with the strong creamy cheese in one bite.

Misha asked many personal questions about our prewar status. Iboya explained that our father had had a shoe business. He made custom and orthopedic shoes, and sold ready-made shoes, too. Iboya used the word "*Geschäft.*" Misha's German was not very good, and she exclaimed, "You owned a factory!" She suddenly looked at us with great respect, and cut us each another slice of bread. Iboya did not correct the confusion.

I ate my second slice slowly, savoring each morsel. Nourished by the food, I felt hope—more than other times when we had heard rumors. I said, "Iboya, maybe this time it's true and we'll be going home."

"I wouldn't go back to Poland. Maybe I will go with you to Hungary," Misha mused. "I have no family left. I made many enemies during the war. Blockovas are misunderstood." Misha seemed as starved for conversation as we were for food.

Back in our barrack now, we gave up looking for the three Hollanders and just settled down near the entrance, next to our blockova Vera's partition. Her quarters were usually quiet at this hour, but tonight there were voices and movement. We concentrated and could distinguish German male voices. Someone said, "The English are but hours away . . . tanks could reach here by morning." He sounded like an SS man.

I turned to Iboya and saw in the darkness a spark in her eyes. "You see, it's really true," I whispered. Iboya nudged me to look up. Two large strapping men, with their heads shorn, wearing clean prisoner uniforms, emerged from Vera's partition, laughing. They were followed by Mindi, a tall, big-boned, yet pretty Romanian girl, who was holding a pair of barber's clippers. She had a bad reputation, even back in Christianstadt, where she traded favors with the male inmates in the ammunition factory. When we first arrived in Bergen-Belsen, we used to hear Mindi return in the middle of the night to give her sisters the food she got from the SS. I was disgusted, but envious. Now, in spite of all that, I was horrified to see that she would go so far as to help the SS disguise themselves as prisoners in order to escape. But Iboya said, "We cannot blame her. Today's bread is certain. Who knows about tomorrow."

There was no roll call the next morning—we were awakened by distant gunfire. With a burst of newfound energy, we rushed out in the dim light to watch the exchange of fire between the fleeing Germans and the approaching British army. I ran up to the gate, praying that this would be the end of our imprisonment. Male prisoners filtered in through the clusters of women, some speaking excitedly, others crying. A few stood repeating the Shema—"Hear, O Israel, the Lord our God, the Lord is One"—not in the traditional way of the prayer, but in demanding voices, calling on God to witness the confrontation with their despairing, wasted women. My grandmother Babi told us children not to use the Lord's name in anger, and it frightened me to hear their chant. Though I didn't always believe in God, I now scanned the sky for bolts of lightning.

The men looked worse than we did. They shouted over one another, telling us who they were, asking where we were from. Husbands, sons, brothers, fathers. They were looking for Hana, Sara, Frida, Bella, Samu, Fage . . . The names were endless.

One woman flew into a man's arms, almost knocking him off his shaking legs. "Miksha, it's me, Ema!" He kissed her without recognition. She pulled away. "Oh, God, you don't recognize me. It's all right," she soothed him, "as long as we are together." Crying and laughing all at once, she pressed up against the bewildered, skeletal form. Then she announced, "This is my husband." Pride and joy shone on her tear- and dirt-streaked face.

I watched other reunions, and listened to the disappointed chanting Kaddish, the prayer for the dead.

Iboya came over to where I stood, pulling a man by the hand. "Look who I found—Pali Ligeti." He had on a pair of German boots that came up over his knees and looked as if they outweighed him. He wore the same filthy blue-and-white-striped uniform as many of the other men, a cap cut out of the same fabric, a few days' worth of stubble that could not conceal the hollows of his face—just the blue of his eyes looked familiar to me. His cold, bony fingers stroked my cheek. "*Szervus Piri.*" I was overcome with emotion, and I wanted to ask about the other men of Beregszász but was afraid.

"He doesn't know of any other men from home, but he'll ask around." Iboya answered the question in my eyes.

"Come, walk back with me; I have some gold bracelets for you," Pali said.

I looked at my scrawny wrist and then at Iboya.

"Go on, it's all right; he will bring you back," she said. "We are safe; the Germans have fled."

I watched Pali make the effort of walking like a man, his shoulder bones like knobs pushing up his uniform, his head half hidden under the cap. "Am I walking too fast for you?" he asked. Without waiting for an answer, he took my hand and led me through the gate to his camp. The milling sound of the prisoners was punctuated by gunshots from the near-distance.

When we reached his barrack, he walked inside ahead of me. "On your guard, men, I'm bringing in a lady; cover yourselves up and watch your language." I looked about the rows of triple bunks. The inmates were hanging over the wood frames. Some, attempting to act civilized, pulled on rags to cover up their bones. One called back to Pali, "We want to watch. It has been a long time, but I bet you can't get it up, either." Laughter followed.

"Come on, Pali, let's see your stuff. Show us how a *Muskelmann* does it," a voice called over my head.

"I told you to clean it up, you pigs, don't you have any manners?" He turned to me apologetically. "They have forgotten how to be gentlemen."

Pali was playing ladies and gentlemen in a tunnel of dying men. I wanted the men to go on laughing at him; he was ridiculous. He pushed a man sprawled over a lower bunk, more dead than alive. "Hershi, move over. They are gone; we are about to be liberated." Barely opening his eyes, Hershi dragged his body away from the edge so Pali could step up and get a bundle from the upper bunk.

Pali could not bend his knees in the German's tall boots. Annoyed, he sat down and pulled them off. Looking at the black, sturdy boots, I imagined their former owner having them shined every morning while he shaved and showered with warm water, put on clean underwear, a crisp white shirt, and the well-tailored SS uniform. He would admire himself in the mirror, eat a nourishing breakfast, then go out to do his daily killing.

Pali finally uncovered a small bundle from its hiding place. Relieved, he climbed down and sat by Hershi. "Hold on, Hershi, hold on," he said, and looked up, remembering that I was waiting.

I watched Pali's feet as he rewrapped them in rags. They were calloused and bruised, with new bloody abrasions from the boots. He shoved his twisted toes back inside them and said, "Come, let's get out of here."

I followed him out of the dark barrack. The air outside made me aware of the smell of decay we left behind. Pali untied the bundle and slipped three gold bracelets over my hand. "I found them inside the boots," he said. They slid off and fell to the ground. He picked them up and shoved them high up on my arm. "You'll grow into them."

When we were in the ghetto in Beregszász, Pali managed to stay in the city by getting himself a job in a bakery. He dashed in on two occasions with a loaf of bread for us and then vanished. Mother told me, "If you stick with him you'll never go hungry."

As we walked back toward the women's camp, we were jostled by swarms of people running in the opposite direction to raid the kitchen. A handful of guards remained—here and there, a prisoner would fall to the ground, hit by a bullet. Momentary screams were heard. Pali guided me to the corner of the gate and pushed me through. "I'll take you to Iboya and then go look for some food."

But Iboya was nowhere to be found. Pali parked me by the entrance of our barrack and said he'd be back. Every shot I heard made me jump and pray that it wasn't my sister who had fallen and been trampled by the crowds. Even the inhabitants of the infirmary crawled out or slid on their stomachs in their rush for freedom. Some of the prisoners had come back from the kitchen with potatoes and were building small fires to bake them. A woman from the infirmary crawled over to a fire, reached in, grabbed a potato from the flames, and devoured it from her scorched hand.

Iboya finally arrived, full of excitement, and pulled out of her bosom several potatoes and an onion. Mrs. Hollander was with her, carrying a pot, her face flushed. Her two daughters, Elza and Magda, gathered some twigs and lit them from a nearby fire. While the potatoes and onion simmered, with Mrs. Hollander tending them, the chaos continued around us. We shared the stew, seated by the fire. When the pot was empty, Mrs. Hollander lay down in the sun. She never woke up. Iboya and I helped Elza and Magda carry her body over to the large heap of decomposing corpses in the back of our barrack. Our line of five was broken, but Mrs. Hollander had gotten her wish. All through our torturous march from Christianstadt to Bergen-Belsen in the blizzards of snow, she kept repeating, "I want to live long enough to feed my daughters just once more and then I will die happy."

Exhausted, I sat down propped against the south wall of the barrack while Iboya went off talking with some people. The April morning sun felt warm, and I dozed off. Toward midafternoon, I was awakened by a tumultuous uproar. The first British tanks approached our gate. They were halted by the mass of prisoners that ran to greet them. I joined the welcomers.

Under their flat caps the eyes and faces of the soldiers registered shock and horror as they stood in the tanks and looked us over. Many hands reached toward them and voices begged for food. English, German, Hungarian, Polish, Dutch, Czech, Romanian, and other languages blended in the shouting.

The soldiers dispensed their rations, giving all that they had on them. Then they pleaded with us to quiet down so we could communicate. They selected an English-speaking prisoner to be the spokesman. He translated in German that we would all be fed very shortly and given medical aid. The crowd slowly dispersed and let the tanks enter our camp.

When Iboya found me back where she had left me, she showed off a tin of preserved meat and a can of evaporated milk that she got from the English soldiers. She pierced the can of milk by hammering a small sharp stone with a rock, and insisted that I drink most of it. Carefully repeating the process, we managed to open the tin. We picked out the spiced meat with our fingers and watched the camp fill with soldiers. Some of them had cameras and took pictures. Then they discovered the stacks of corpses behind the barracks and brought out movie cameras. When the Germans realized they were losing the war, they had stopped hiding their victims.

Iboya and I lined up with the groups in front of the ten-foot-high stacks being filmed. I hoped that I would be discovered by a lost member of our family. A Yiddish-speaking English soldier who asked us questions said, "This film will be shown in newsreels, so the world will know what has taken place." He was crying. "My dear children, your suffering must be known."

I was gratified by his emotion, and a new feeling surfaced inside me—a sense of importance, that we mattered to the outside world. My eyes welled with tears and suddenly I was sobbing. The soldier came over and embraced me, taking no notice of my dirty appearance and lice-infested clothes. He asked my name.

"Piri," I answered.
"How old are you, Piri?"
"Almost fifteen."
One of the cameramen tapped him on the shoulder and told him to move on. He searched his pockets for something to give me. Finding only cigarettes, he took the whistle from around his neck and hung it on mine.
Soon after he left, I heard strange music that sounded like whining flutes. Looking toward it, I saw a group wearing pleated skirts and carrying complicated instruments. They were men. We all surrounded them. I stifled my giggles, not wanting to insult them, but the other prisoners were laughing without reserve. It did not seem to faze the musicians; they continued playing in utmost earnest. Finishing their piece, they proceeded to organize us into two rows facing each other, and then moved between the rows demonstrating the steps to the hokey-pokey. Imitating their gestures, we raised our arms and bumped our hips. The words were difficult, but we put all our effort into singing along.
I got dizzy after a while and stood to the side observing. A man next to me explained that the musicians were Scottish, wearing their national costume and playing the traditional bagpipes. Iboya joined us, looking me over. "I think you've had enough for one day," she said.
As we wandered toward our barrack, my stomach started to cramp and bubble. I suffered with diarrhea all night. "It is my fault," Iboya said remorsefully. "I should not have fed you the rich preserved foods, but I thought they would give you strength."
By morning I was too weak to stand up. Iboya carried me over to the door so I could get some air, then went in search of help. She came back dragging a medic and pleading, "My sister is dying. You must take her or it will be too late."

The soldier checked my pulse and marked my forehead with a red cross. As soon as he turned his head, Iboya knelt down beside me. She moistened the red mark with spittle and pressed her forehead like a blotter over mine. "I'm not going to let them separate us now," she whispered. When they came to put me on a stretcher, she lay down on it alongside me.

2

I awoke tossing in my bed, the covers kicked off, exposing my emaciated body. Sunlight filled the stark white hospital room. Iboya was standing over me.

"*Gots viln!* I think Piri's fever broke, her forehead feels cool." Turning to the girl in the next bed, she asked, "Would you watch her for a few minutes?"

Iboya came back with a doctor. He checked my pulse and declared, almost shouting in his excitement, "The fever is over! I knew you were a fighter. How do you feel?"

I was uncertain about speaking. Instead of answering, I looked at each of the three faces smiling down at me, all of them now clear, without the veil of fever. The man in white was surprisingly young and very handsome. I recalled glimpses of him hovering over me, his face intent, his large hands heavy and gentle all at the same time. He had seemed a fatherly, middle-aged man to me. Who was he, to have cared so much about my recovery?

The blue-eyed girl standing next to him said, "My name is Lyral." I remembered her feeding me smooth grape sugar in the stillness of night.

Iboya kept repeating, "You're well, it's over, we'll be going home together." It sounded more like a prayer of gratitude than a promise or conviction.

The doctor was removing a small tube from my arm. "Piri, you have been a very sick girl," he said. "You had us pretty worried. Typhoid, dysentery, and of course malnutrition. Your fever lasted over two weeks. You don't remember too much of it, do you?" He pushed aside a stand with an upside-down bottle. "You will not need this anymore—time for some real food."

Finding my voice now, I said, "I do feel hungry." The laughter around me sounded like a burst of spontaneous applause. Lyral brought the pillow from her bed and tenderly propped me up to a sitting position, while Iboya fed me clear broth and gelatin.

Mindi and her two younger sisters came over to witness my first meal in the hospital. I had been aware of their presence in the ward—mainly of Mindi's pleading and fighting with the doctors for an abortion. "I'm not taking an SS bastard child home with me," she had shouted one day. "I'm only twenty. I want to start a new life." Her sisters tried to quiet her in their embarrassment. "Who did I do it for, if not to save you from starvation? This is the thanks I get. Suddenly you can afford the luxury of shame."

My eyes were drawn from the food I was eating to Mindi's stomach. It did not protrude yet.

The ward was silent the day Mindi was taken to the operating room. We all looked at her empty bed, waiting. Her sisters kept busy on the floor, cutting large circles out of a blanket for skirts and wrapping the pieces of gray flannel about their waists for a fitting. They were readying themselves to become civilians, to cast away their hospital shirts along with their pasts. I watched their needles pierce the thick flannel with determination, feeling that I had a long way to go.

When Mindi was finally wheeled back, the silence

seemed to grow louder and the needles poised in midair. Only the movements of the nurses could be heard in the room. Mindi, asleep, was lifted and gently tucked in her bed. Her sisters dropped their sewing and stood over her.

It was one of Lyral's mournful French songs that broke the silence. The words were foreign, but the melody was familiar, remembered by all of us from our childhood.

A week later I walked down the long white corridor, supported by Iboya and Lyral, and looked into the rooms filled with metal beds. We stopped at the nurses' station to show off my progress to the volunteer medical staff. The young Belgian doctor came out from the inner office to congratulate me, his face filled with pride.

He asked me to walk back unaided and crossed his arms over his chest as he watched. I wanted to walk erect to show him my recovery, but at the same time, I felt naked under the light, transparent night shirt. I wished for a bathrobe to conceal my silhouette, and found myself running on wobbly legs till I collapsed over my bed in a fit of sobs.

Lyral came to my side. The doctor followed Iboya into our room and, seeing Lyral comforting me, quietly backed out. In hushed tones, Lyral talked to me about her home in Paris. Her voice had notes of music even in speech. I loved listening to her and soon stopped crying.

I visualized two picture-postcard images; the Arc de Triomphe and the Eiffel Tower. I could not imagine private homes, yet Lyral spoke of a two-family house where she had lived with her mother and her little girl, Irma, before the Germans picked her up. She also described small shops and a church where her mother, who had a bad heart, was always stopping in to pray.

"Aren't you Jewish?" I asked her.
"No, I'm Catholic."
"Then why are you here?"
"I was a messenger in the French Resistance."
I was going to tell Lyral about the political prisoners working in the ammunition factory in Christianstadt, but Mindi, by now recovered from her abortion, walked over and sat down on the next bed. "How old is your little girl?" she asked, folding her hands over her stomach.
"She should be five years old," said Lyral with a sigh. The four of us sat in silence, each hoping that the child was safe.
After sending several letters to try to locate her mother, her child, and her boyfriend André, Lyral received a reply. It was from André's companion in the Resistance, Roget, with the return address of the Café du Quai, where Lyral had worked as a singer. Mindi, her two sisters, Iboya, and I crowded around Lyral's bed while she ripped the letter open. Her eyes moved quickly down the page, blinking away tears. Putting the letter back in the envelope, she looked up, shaking her head. "He has no news of André and does not know the whereabouts of Mama and Irma. They fled Paris right after I was taken to prison." Lyral put the letter under her pillow and curled up in a fetal position. Pulling the covers over her, Iboya asked, "Does he know if André was picked up and taken to Germany?"
"They both were, but Roget came back."
The three sisters walked to their side of the ward. I lay down on my bed. Iboya, sitting by Lyral's side, patted her back in a soothing rhythm.

Lyral was the first to leave the hospital. She gave us the address of the café, saying, "Keep in touch from wherever you decide to go." She seemed happy and excited, but we cried over losing her and over our own uncertain futures.

At the end of May, when I was able to walk about the grounds, clothing came from the American Jewish charities. We were each allowed to pick one outfit. I selected a large dress and sweater that I could give to Mother. I was lost in them. Iboya turned to look at me and started to cry, because she had done the same thing. The woman in charge made us pick out clothes more suitable for our small frames, but Iboya held on to her sweater and would not give it up.

We met friends on the road who had worked with us in the kitchen in Christianstadt, and they invited us to their apartment near the hospital, which had been deserted by its German occupants. Sitting around their porch sucking on sugar cubes and sipping tea, we discussed our plans. One angry young woman said, "Why go back to our countries? They threw us out, sold us to Hitler for ammunition."

"Because we must go home," I insisted.

"There is no home for Jews," she said. "Maybe Palestine, but the British are there and won't let us immigrate."

So where? Iboya and I pondered the question on our way back to the hospital without resolve.

A few days later, a woman from the Red Cross came to interview us. "Since Piri is still sickly," she said, "the Swedish Red Cross will take you in."

Iboya agreed with great relief, but I was hysterical. "I want to go home. How else will we find the others? They will go back and we won't be there. They will never know what happened to us."

"Piri, while you were sick I was speaking to a lot of

people," said Iboya. "From all that I've heard, there are no others. Thank God, we have another place to go to. In Sweden, they will make you well."

I didn't answer her.

"Piri, you aren't listening," Iboya snapped.

She was right. But in spite of not wanting to listen to Iboya, I knew that I would have to do whatever she decided.

It was just after my fifteenth birthday, toward the middle of June, when the Red Cross lady reappeared. Iboya and I were still in bed. Leaning against the washstand dividing our beds, she announced, "You will be starting your journey for Sweden right after breakfast."

We both sat up, wide awake.

Her face deflated. "Don't you want to go?"

"Of course," Iboya tried to assure her. "We just aren't ready." Iboya turned to me to back her up. "Right, Piri?"

"What is Sweden like?" I asked.

"A country not touched by war, where life will be good for you." I could not imagine such a place. "You'll have everything you need to make you well. The Swedes are great people." She mussed my short hair. "Come on! Put on your clothes. You'll have breakfast and get started." While Iboya and I dressed, she lifted our medical charts off the ends of our beds. Then she walked us toward the door. The three Romanian sisters looked on enviously. On an impulse, we turned to hug them.

"Maybe we'll meet again . . ." I said, knowing too well that we never would, and not sure that it mattered. We just needed to embrace someone before leaving that part of our lives behind.

In the dining hall, we met many other patients who would be traveling with us. Some of them were talking excitedly around the tables. Others, like me, sat quietly. We got a short briefing from the Red Cross lady. "You will start your journey by train to Lübeck, a seaport in Germany. From there, you will sail on a boat to Halsingborg, your first stop in Sweden."

As we lined up in the hall, I realized that the Red Cross lady and some of the medical staff from the hospital would accompany us. My thoughts turned to the young Belgian doctor. I got out of line and started for his office. The Red Cross lady tried to stop me. "Where do you think you're going?"

"I must say goodbye to my doctor," I insisted, and ran back down the long corridor, where he and I met head-on. Suddenly I lost my nerve.

"I was just coming to see you off," the doctor said.

I wanted to reach out and hug him, but he stood so tall and big, and the Red Cross lady was watching. "Why aren't you coming with us?" I managed to ask, and was choked by tears.

"You won't need me. There are many good doctors in Sweden." I finally allowed myself to look up at his face and was surprised to see that his warm brown eyes, too, were moist with tears.

"Goodbye, Piri. Be a good girl. Get yourself strong and healthy."

He pulled me close to him, then let go. I felt empty; all words of gratitude escaped me. The Red Cross lady, understanding, put her arm around me, leading me away. I turned to wave. He waved back.

I had the upper berth on the train, and watched the vegetation dotted with burned-out ruins fly by. From time to time I dozed. It turned dark and I slept through a whole night.

We got off the train in broad daylight. A big white house stood in the distance, enclosed by a wire fence. We walked toward it, but were stopped short in front of a tunnel of tents on the lawn. Inside them several Red Cross women formed an assembly line. We were told to undress, and our short hair was dosed with disinfectant. Then we were given clothes from big piles. When we emerged at the other end of the tunnel, we were transformed. I was wearing a red wool dress much too hot for June. Iboya was wearing navy slacks that had a fly front she had neglected to close. There was a burst of laughter, and she blushed scarlet searching for the buttons. She was still holding on to the large sweater, I noticed.

In the big house, we were served mounds of white bread that had a crunchy crust with a fluffy center, red jam, and large pitchers of real milk. It was the first time that we could eat as much as we wanted. After countless slices spread thickly with the red jam, and several glasses of milk, I felt content and reassured that the Red Cross lady had told the truth about life in Sweden being good for us.

The first morning after our arrival in Lübeck, the Red Cross lady encouraged us to go out. "Take large breaths of sea air. It is a gorgeous day." Walking down the path, I noticed a very pretty girl in a light print dress standing by herself. Her dark brown straight hair, short like ours, was growing in uneven wisps. But on her, it was becoming, sort of pixieish. She was staring out toward the sea with a melancholy look I could relate to. "Let's ask her to walk with us," I was about to suggest, when I realized that Iboya was already going toward her.

"*Szervus,*" Iboya greeted her.

She turned, taken by surprise, but did not answer.

"The water is really blue," Iboya persisted, and I saw that the two large eyes looking us over were the same shade of blue as the sea.

"Would you like to walk with us? I'm Iboya Davidowitz, and this is my sister Piri."

"Mine is Dora—Dora Morgen." She told us that she was from Budapest. I had already guessed as much from her elegant posture and speech.

After that first meeting, we walked and talked every chance we had inside the wire-enclosed compound, and became good friends.

On the day of our departure, after a two-week stay, I stood with Iboya and Dora looking around the busy pier at Lübeck harbor. Suddenly I spotted Pali waving to me from the ship we were about to board. He had gained weight and looked more like the young man I knew in Beregszász, the one who had once serenaded me under my bedroom window. I had not seen him since the day we were liberated.

As soon as we boarded, Pali pushed through the crowd and hugged me exuberantly.

"Where are your boots?" I asked him, wriggling out of his grasp.

"Oh, those; I got better ones." He motioned to a pair of brown oxfords that he wore. "I came back looking for you the next day with all kinds of things, but you were gone. Some of us men walked into the city and looted a deserted house."

Iboya took over the conversation. "I got some canned meat and condensed milk from the English soldiers and gave it to Piri. She got violently sick and was one of the first ones to be taken to the hospital."

"Do you have the bracelets I gave you?" Pali asked. My mind flashed back to the bath I was given on my way to the hospital by a German woman with a Red Cross armband. She sponged me on top of a high table, asking many questions. I was very feverish. She seemed sympathetic. She had taken off the bracelets to bathe me and that was the last time I had seen them.

"No," I answered him. "I lost them on my way to the hospital."

"Too bad. You could have gotten some money for them," Pali said, shaking his head. "Enough of that. I'd like you to meet my friend Hershi."

The young man next to him extended his hand. "We met before, but you don't remember me. I had the bunk under Pali's. I saw you when you came in." This handsome young man with curly red hair was the skeleton that rolled over moaning in pain?

He chuckled, reading my surprise. "Pali nursed me back to health."

Hershi told us about an aunt and a cousin he had found in Bergen-Belsen who were on the boat, and we all went down to see them in the bottom of the ship, which was fixed up as a hospital. We stopped at their beds and Hershi introduced us to a middle-aged woman and a young girl about seventeen. Iboya and I made our usual search among the patients and asked questions, in hopes of finding our sister Rozsi or another missing member of our family. Dora did the same, but we met with disappointment. We went back up on the deck and stayed there for the rest of our boat ride, talking and anxiously awaiting the shores of Halsingborg.

We arrived late in the afternoon, to a heavy traffic of bicycles mixed with some automobiles. It seemed at first as though the entire population of the city had come out to greet us. We later found out that they were coming home from work, and when they saw the procession of open trucks that we were traveling in, a lot of them filed behind us out of curiosity.

One woman pedaled her bicycle very close to our truck and tried to keep up a conversation with us in Yiddish. "I got out of Poland just in time, but not my parents. Are there any Polish Jews among you?" she asked. Another woman yelled back information in Polish.

When our truck stopped, the bicyclist was there, offering her services as a translator. The attending staff of the Swedish Red Cross was glad to have her. They were overwhelmed and unprepared, expecting to have us stand in line and patiently await our turn, while they gave us medical examinations that would determine our next stop. But we were barely two months out of the concentration camps and not ready to trust strangers to make decisions for us. The doctors and nurses were worn out but wiser by the time they finished examining and sorting us. The very sick were taken to a hospital, and the remaining men and women were put on two separate trucks going in different directions.

The second stop in Sweden for Iboya, Dora, and me was a quarantine in Hoganas, a convalescent home.

Again we were fenced in by wire—to keep us away from the civilians, in case we carried contagious diseases. Every day a huge crowd of onlookers gathered around the fence. They had seen the newsreels of the camps and read about us in their newspapers, and now they came to see us. Some spoke German and tried to talk to us. By the second week, it became sort of a contest to meet them at the fence, and see if any would address us personally. We all loved the attention. Sometimes they would throw over little gifts. In spite of its being forbidden, we would accept them. A dashing blond young man in an air force uniform had begun to stop by. He would address all of his remarks to our little group of three. One day he wrote something on a toy tennis racket and threw it over the fence. We grabbed for it. In German he had written "I love you." We were unsure which one of us he had in mind and he never let on. When his furlough was over and he stopped coming, we each felt a loss.

After a month's observation, we were allowed to visit with Swedish families on Sundays. Iboya, Dora, and I were invited for Sunday dinner to the home of a family with two children, a boy about twelve and a girl, nine. The husband and wife spoke a little German and could manage some conversation. Here was a family intact in their own home, within their own country. Dora, as far as she knew, was the only one left of a family of four. Iboya and I were two from a family of nine.

During dinner the children urged us to eat, in sign language. "They have heard that you had no food," the father explained. Next they took part of their dinner off their plates and put it on ours. At this the mother and father exchanged proud glances. But we were no longer starved for food.

For a moment, as I looked around the dining room at the father and mother and two innocent children, my mind went back to our kitchen in Beregszász and I saw Mother in her Sabbath dress, Father in his gray suit, freshly shaved, cutting the challah and passing the slices, one by one, to Lilli, Lajos, Rozsi, Etu, Iboya, Sandor, Manci, and Joli.

The children's Swedish chatter brought me back to reality. Was it just the chance of geography that had made our lives so different, I wondered. I hated myself for looking at them in envy and resentment. They meant so well, but I declined the next time they came to take us out.

By the third month of quarantine, we had recovered most of our strength, and with it came a restlessness. Iboya, Dora, and I pleaded one day with Fru Banson, the woman in charge, to let us go into town unescorted. After much persuasion, she said, "You can leave after dinner and stay out till supper, but you must be on your best behavior!" Overjoyed, we walked, ran, and skipped aimlessly through the streets until we reached a square with many impressive shops that seemed to be the center of Hoganas. Looking into the windows, we fantasized about which dress, blouse, skirt, or shoes we might have bought if we had the money. We were bent over, with our noses pressed up against the window of a dress shop, when it started to rain. Splashed by large raindrops, we scrambled up to the threshold of the store to keep from getting soaked. A young saleswoman opened the door to let us in, which startled us. An older woman behind the counter smiled to put us at ease, and asked us to enter. She motioned for us to come closer, and made an attempt to converse with us. By now, we had learned to understand "*stackars flickar*"—poor girls—a reference to us that was used over and over, with the deep inhaled sighs that only the Swedes can make.

We decided to try our limited Swedish vocabulary.

"We are refugees, we live at a convalescent home, and we can't speak much Swedish. Sweden very nice, people nice; we are Hungarian, came from Germany." They both acknowledged each piece of information. "*Ja, ja, vi förstår*"—we understand—"*stackars flickar.*" More smiles, more sighs. The older woman studied us for size and took some boxes off the shelves behind her. Lifting out three pretty blouses, she came around the counter, held them up to our shoulders, and gave them to us. Our opinion of the Swedish people was pretty special—they had been extremely caring and generous toward us ever since our arrival, but to give us brand-new blouses . . . We were overcome with gratitude. "*Tack såa mycket,*" we all said simultaneously.

During the quarantine we had each acquired two changes of clothing and a fairly comfortable pair of shoes, but all of it was secondhand. A new blouse without a former owner was something else entirely. I could hardly wait to try mine on. It was a loose weave like natural linen, with a navy and red geometric design. Iboya's was yellow with blue and green, Dora's solid pink. I think the lady tried to complement our coloring.

Running back home, we jumped into puddles and yelled, "Yippee." Suddenly Iboya stopped. "How will we explain the gifts to Fru Banson? She might think we stole them or begged for them. She won't let us go next time."

"We can't hide them," Dora said. "That will look worse."

Dora offered to do the explaining, but Fru Banson let it pass, with a lecture about not accepting gifts again. We were allowed to go out on a few more occasions, but not as a threesome.

Early in September, shortly after our day of adventure, Dora was sent off to a school specially set up for child survivors. Iboya, too, was picked to go with this group, but refused to leave unless I was allowed to join them. Having maneuvered out of three major separations in Auschwitz when the Germans made their periodic selections for the gas chambers, we found the very idea of separating from each other unthinkable. Fru Banson sat us down and explained that "*Stackars Piri*" was left with a heart murmur from the lengthy trauma of high fever and needed more rest under medical supervision. But she permitted Iboya to remain with me.

Dora wrote as soon as she had settled in. Her first letter was addressed in Hungarian to both of us, but Iboya gave it to me. "Go ahead and open it; she is really your friend. You two have more in common." I was not very surprised at Iboya's attitude. She had assumed the role of big sister to both Dora and me ever since we arrived at the quarantine. Actually, Dora was Iboya's age, but that did not seem to matter.

Dear Iboya and Piri,

Visingso is a beautiful island. The school is a converted summer camp. Kitchen, dining hall, and staff quarters are in a large white house. The students are divided up into six low barrack-like structures. Two others serve as classrooms.

The best part about being in school is that we are all around the same age (between sixteen and eighteen)—too bad mostly girls. I feel more comfortable with them than with the older women at the quarantine. The women's constant talk about home and never-ending chatter about food and recipes used to make me want to scream.

Of course, the transition from idle patients to students with homework will take some adjustment—mainly, learning to concentrate again. We were given tests to find out where we left off in math, reading, and composition. I was shocked to find out how much I had forgotten.

I hope you two will be joining me shortly. I miss you.

Write back soon.

Love,
Dora

Instead of following Dora to Visingso, Iboya and I were sent to another convalescent facility in Robertshojd. It was also a summer camp converted to house survivors who were not yet ready to be placed in the job market. It was staffed mostly with Swedish volunteers, all kind, motherly figures. The lady in charge was Fru Matson—tall, efficient, always on the run between the long cabins where we lived and the main house, where she had her office.

Fru Matson was never too busy to stop and listen to any of our needs. She spoke to us in Swedish, and German if need be. We were free to roam about. The staff also tried to fill our time by providing books, and an occasional film would be shown.

One evening they acquired an old Hungarian movie. In the dining-hall-turned-cinema, over a hundred of us gathered together. Fru Matson also invited the camp from two miles down the road, which added another hundred women and some thirty men. Mingling with the other campers, Iboya and I thought we recognized our older sister Rozsi's friend from Komjaty. As soon as we started to explain that she looked familiar, she interrupted, "Yes, I'm Suri and you are Fage Neni's granddaughters, and Rozsi, is she . . ."

"No," we both answered.

Iboya broke the silence. "You should know more about Rozsi than we, since you must have gone to Auschwitz together from the ghetto."

Suri's eyes lingered on us with sympathy. "I don't know—or remember—anything. It is all mixed up like a bad dream. I could not tell you what happened to my own mother. People vanished. That's all I will ever know, *Gotenyu.*" She spoke in Yiddish, wrapping the words in sighs. We asked no more, just made ordinary conversation and watched the others milling about, looking each other over, getting excited, apologizing, and walking away.

Fru Matson announced, "Take your seats, the film is about to begin."

All whispering and shuffling of chairs stopped as the sound burst forth from the projector.

I watched and listened in a stupor, not following the story. The black-and-white figures were just silhouettes moving across the screen, yet I was moved to tears. My head ached, my chest heaved, and the screen became a blur. I looked at Iboya next to me. She was rigid, with her shoulders pulled up toward her ears and her eyes staring straight ahead.

When the film was over, we walked back to our quarters, and as soon as we entered our room, I threw myself on my bed and cried, "I want to go home." I sobbed, and talked incoherently about returning to Hungary. Iboya tried to reason with me, but I refused to hear her words.

The other four women we shared the large room with slowly drifted in. The oldest of them stopped at Iboya's side and said, "Leave her be, let her cry it out." It turned out to be a bad night for everybody.

We had no East European films after that. Instead, they took us on occasion to a local movie house, where we saw Swedish and sometimes American movies. One of the women among us was a former dance teacher and volunteered to give us dance exercises. Some of the women had had previous training, and they reminisced during class.

Iboya and I often walked to the nearby camp and visited Suri. She was trying to locate her relatives in America. "I would not go back to Komjaty if they paid me," she once told us. "They couldn't wait to get rid of us, so we would leave behind what little we owned and they could grab it."

"You mean the peasants, like my Babi's neighbors?" I asked in shock.

"Piri, you were a little girl there on a summer's holiday. You saw them as a visitor. You know we are all on our best behavior in front of company."

"But my Babi said they were her friends."

"Your Babi, God rest her soul, was a very religious woman. She could see only the good in people."

I wanted to protest, but suddenly remembered the time when my two girlfriends back in the city, Vali and Milush, told me in whispers how they were planning to move into the big house where their mother had worked as a domestic. "We are not to tell anyone, but our mother told us that after the Jews are taken away, we will move into the Schwartzes' house." I had put it out of my mind, dismissing it as one of our games of make-believe, like playing house. Recalling it now, I wondered if that was the reason for my not writing to them after the war. I felt depressed.

Iboya was urging Suri, "If you should find your relatives in America and be able to emigrate, please help us to look for ours. You have more information than we do. We can't remember any of our four uncles' addresses."

As November approached, we got our first taste of a Swedish winter. It turned so bitter cold it became an effort to get about. The ground was frozen, and the wind slashed freely in the open space outside. Soon snow covered our campsite. We seldom made the journey to visit Suri now. Inside our poorly insulated quarters, we slept with several blankets piled on us, exposing only the top of our heads.

One December night the six of us were awakened from sleep to witness a terrifying scene. Four women in long white shrouds were walking between our beds, with candles flaming around their heads. They were carrying trays. In the doorway stood a dark figure topped by a tall hat, holding a long torch. Two of my roommates pulled their covers over their faces, while I sprang up into a sitting position ready to run. The women in white kept circling our beds, singing in unison a Swedish chant, while the guard stood motionless. The candles burned in a steady glow, lighting up the dark of the night. As one of the women lowered her tray to me, I jumped off my bed and almost knocked the tray down. Looking back over my shoulder, I recognized her as one of the young kitchen helpers. Her familiar face put me at ease. Without halting in her singing, she steadied the tray and gestured for me to help myself. On it were cups of steaming coffee and braided saffron buns. I took one of the cups and a bun and sat down on my bed. Iboya, in the bed next to mine, did the same. In silence we sipped and munched. When we were all served, the guard entered, and it turned out to be Fru Matson. We applauded in delight.

She explained to us that this was an old Swedish custom, called Santa Lucia Eve—the Festival of Lights. "Every December 13, we celebrate the return of more daylight hours to the dark Swedish winter. These girls in white represent Santa Lucia. Usually the oldest unmarried daughter will rise early before daybreak and serve coffee and buns to her family. The guard is usually a man, but we had no man volunteering, so I put on the costume."

On closer examination I could see that the candles were secured on a halo-like circular wire which had small candleholders equally spaced and was decorated with snips of lingonberry branches. After we drank and ate ourselves awake, the women taught us the song of Santa Lucia.

Santa Lucia,
Thy light is glowing
Through darkest winter night,
Comfort bestowing.
Dreams float on wings bedight,
Comes then the morning light,
Santa Lucia,
Santa Lucia.

Beginning with that night, the Swedish Christmas season continued on into January. Unfortunately, I missed most of the festivities by getting sick and having to stay in the hospital for two weeks. My stomach rejected the rich traditional foods. Dr. Moser, who was in charge of me in the hospital, told Iboya that my ailment was due to my weakened intestinal tract from the typhoid and dysentery. Iboya came to visit me every day. Often one of our roommates or Suri would accompany her.

We kept in touch with Dora by correspondence for almost four months. It was not until the middle of January that Iboya and I were able to join her. On a blustery winter day we left Robertshojd, accompanied by a caseworker. We traveled by train to Granna, the nearest land stop to Dora's school on the island of Visingso, and were put up in a hotel. Because we had arrived in the dead of winter, and the island, usually reached by boat, was now surrounded by rapidly freezing water, we would be able to cross it only by sled. Each day the two men in charge of pulling the sled would check and measure the ice for safety, while we watched the blizzards through a frosted window that looked out on the island. It seemed like a long distance between the shore and Visingso. Neither the big main house nor the long barracks Dora wrote about could be seen. Finally, on the seventh day of our stay in the hotel, we were told to rise at 5:00 A.M. because we would be making the journey. After a rushed breakfast Iboya and I were bundled into blankets and strapped on individual sleds. The two men harnessed themselves and became our sled dogs. By now we could speak Swedish fairly well and understood their concerned conversation about the safety of the crossing. For our benefit, they tried to act confident. "We have made this trip many times before," one of them said, "and the ice is several centimeters thick; there should be no trouble."

Near the shore the ice was solid, but as we progressed, sharp zigzag cracks, like lightning in an electrical storm, were made under our weight. The men looked scared. They decided to distribute the weight by separating. The wind was ruthless, circling the ice and blowing the top layer of snow in our eyes, the only part of us that was exposed. The horizon was vast and empty; the only things breaking the space were our two small sleds. Above the howling wind we heard the periodic crackling of ice. Iboya and I waved to each other for encouragement across the short distance between us, but I had doubts about reaching Visingso alive.

About halfway through, there was a jarring sound as a large jagged piece of ice cracked under us, letting some water flow over the broken chunks. The men quickly maneuvered us back onto solid footing. They also removed our straps in case we had to jump out of the sleds at the next break.

"It won't happen again," the man pulling my sled tried to assure us, "but if the sleds should break away from us, you will be free to jump off and manage for yourselves. Can you girls swim?"

Iboya and I shook our heads no.

"If danger should occur, just lie down on your stomach and hold fast to a chunk of ice." He lay down and demonstrated.

These were not comforting words, but we could not turn back. One side was as risky as the other. Iboya called out, "Would it help if we got off and walked?" They consulted, and let us walk for a while. Our shoes did not have thick soles like their boots did, and our feet, having been badly frozen on the six-week-long march in Germany, were soon numb. We did not refuse when they offered to pull us again. There were only minor cracks on the second half of our trip, and mercifully we arrived without a major incident.

We were greeted with hot chocolate and sweet buns in the main house dining room. The lady in charge was Froken Apt, short and cherubic, with sparkling brown eyes and a nervous manner. She was all concern and attention, both to the two men and to us. She let Iboya and me rest in her own room till lunchtime. "The student quarters are noisy this time of day. Here you can take a nap undisturbed," she explained, removing a black lace nightgown from under the pillow and throwing back the covers on the spacious double bed. After she left the room, we giggled about the flimsy gown and wondered whom she was impressing. Iboya held it up to herself before getting under the covers. The sheets were scented with perfume; we giggled again and fell sound asleep.

We were awakened at noon for *middag,* the main meal of the day, and entered a crowded and noisy dining room. Dora ran over, and all three of us cried with joy. I noticed there were just a few boys in the crowd of girls, reminding me again that females had survived in greater numbers. We sat at the table we were assigned to and were looked over by the curious eyes of both sexes. There was a teacher at either end of the table trying to control the noise. They asked us to introduce ourselves. Herr Weinberg was a good-looking man of about thirty, and Froken Snyder was a pleasant woman a few years younger. Dora later informed us that they were lovers.

After *middag* there was a mail call. I was amazed at how many people received letters, but even more amazed when someone handed me an envelope. Who could know my whereabouts? I was disappointed to see Pali's name with a Stockholm return address. He had tracked us down again through the Swedish Red Cross. I thought he would give up, since I hadn't answered his letter from quarantine. He wrote that he knew about my being taken to the hospital and hoped I was over my vomiting. "The doctor assured me on the telephone that you would make a complete recovery."

I had been hoping the letter would be from one of the lost members of our family. Still, it made me look important to receive mail, and I pretended it was from someone special.

"He called Dr. Moser," I whispered to Iboya.

"He really cares about you," she said with a wink.

"Too bad I don't care about him."

"Well, there are a couple of others to choose from here." She pointed to the group of young men at the ping-pong table looking us over. I had already noticed someone around eighteen or so with shiny black hair and white teeth. He resembled Gari Weiss, Judi Gerber's boyfriend from the ghetto. The reminder was painful, yet I hoped he did not have a girlfriend.

We were shown to our quarters in the same barrack Dora stayed in and were told we would be starting classes tomorrow. Iboya and I were given a small narrow room at the front entrance. Against the right wall was a bunk bed. Directly under the window was a writing table with one chair. The left wall held some shelves, two large hooks, and an old-fashioned chest of drawers topped by a mirror. We hung up our coats and laid our scarves, hats, and gloves on a shelf. The rest of our belongings were to be sent "as soon as possible," the proprietor of the hotel told us, and Froken Apt promised to see about lending us some clothing in the meantime. Iboya told me to slip off my shoes, undress, and get under the blanket. "It's cold in here. All you need is to catch a chill." I climbed up onto the top bunk and looked out the window. Everything was covered in white snow, giving me the feeling that I, too, could erase the past and make a new beginning.

"I'm going to like it here," I said.

"I know," replied Iboya. "You always like the adventure of a new place, and these are our first private quarters since home."

I fell asleep wondering how Iboya could always guess my thoughts.

The better part of our second day was spent in attending classes. We were told by Froken Apt to observe and try to participate in each subject being taught, and that at the end of each period the teachers would ask Iboya and me questions to evaluate our comprehension. The classrooms were in two of the low structures like our living quarters, but there were fewer partitions. Each room contained a blackboard, a desk and chair for the teacher, and rows of old rickety tables and chairs for the students.

We had been delayed by taking our Swedish-language test first and chatting with Herr Jonnson, the Swedish teacher. By the time we approached the open door to the science class, it was in full progress. We found Herr Weinberg throwing a fistful of chalk powder across the surface of the blackboard and watching it cascade down to the wooden floor. His face was flushed with excitement as he declared to his captivated students, "It is foolproof—it will fall down every time!" He faced the class, resembling a magician who had just performed his cleverest trick. I wondered about Herr Weinberg's sanity and turned to Iboya. She shrugged her shoulders and whispered, "I have no idea." We walked in apprehensively. All eyes turned from the blackboard to us.

"You must be the two new girls," Herr Weinberg said,

giving Iboya and me a disagreeable look. "You are late. Find yourselves some chairs." We eased into the back row.

The young man whom I had noticed in the dining room on the first day turned in his seat, which was right in front of mine. "We are learning the laws of gravity," he whispered through those marvelous white teeth. This made no sense to me, but I was dazzled by seeing his face so close to mine.

After writing some numbers and letters on the board, Herr Weinberg smiled invitingly at Iboya and me and asked, "Would one of the new girls like to try solving this one?" I could feel my face burning and heard the word "No" escape from my mouth. There was some snickering. Iboya stood up and waited for it to stop.

"My sister was just released from a hospital and we have never studied anything like this before." The whole class turned to look at us, except the young man in front of me.

"Sorry, I thought you came from another school. Well, never mind, you'll catch up, but I still need a volunteer." Herr Weinberg searched the class and pointed at the only person that wasn't facing us. "David," he called. So that is his name, I thought, and let my eyes follow the self-assured shoulders to the blackboard. He explained the problem in a slow, clear voice as he wrote, but I could not understand the logic behind it. Then he finished and returned to his seat. Everybody copied the problem.

"I want each of you to make up a similar problem for your homework," Herr Weinberg said, looking at his watch. He dismissed the class, then pointed to Iboya and me, saying, "You two will stay."

David spoke to us as he got up. "It really isn't hard once you understand it, and I would be glad to help you if you have any trouble," he offered.

"Thank you," Iboya said before I could manage the words, extending her hand and introducing herself.

I followed her example. "My name is Piri."

"Mine is David."

"I know," I replied, and felt dumb for saying it. David gave me a sympathetic grin, then picked up his books and left.

Herr Weinberg asked me where we had left off in science.

"I never had science. My studies stopped officially when I was twelve," I told him.

"I had some," Iboya said, "but I couldn't follow your class."

He studied her face. "How old are you?"

"I'll be eighteen in May," Iboya confessed shyly.

"And I'll be sixteen in June," I offered.

"Are you well now?" he asked me. "Can you work hard, or would you like to skip my science class?"

"No—I mean, I can work, I feel fine."

"It will be hard, make no mistake about it," he said, half discouraging me, "but if you'd like to give it a try, I'll give you some extra help."

We both answered with an eager "Yes," and Herr Weinberg wrote an example on the board. Iboya understood it; I did not. Handing us a book to share, he said, "Start at the beginning and each of you work as far as you are able. Then we'll see."

A new group of students started to fill the room. "This is my next class. You two might as well stay, and we'll see how you test in math." Dora was among the newcomers and asked us to sit with her.

When everyone was seated, Herr Weinberg drew a cube on the board and wrote the dimensions on its six sides. "We are going to review last week's lesson. Who would like to come to the board and do it?"

Several hands went up, including Dora's. I had a bad moment when Herr Weinberg pointed toward us, till he called Dora's name. I watched Dora take the chalk and start multiplying the numbers, but could not remember the reason for multiplying.

"Try it," Iboya urged me. I copied the numbers in my notebook, but my hand shook and I could not draw a straight line.

"You used to be good in math," Iboya whispered. "It will come back to you."

By the end of the class, I could see things a little clearer, but I tested very low. Addition was the only math that I hadn't forgotten. I felt humiliated. "Your sister can give you some practice problems," Herr Weinberg told me, realizing Iboya's superiority.

We missed the last class. The students were gathering up their books and filing out of the room as Iboya and I approached. Iboya walked straight to the teacher's desk. "I'm sorry we are late. We were detained. We just arrived yesterday and . . ."

"That's all right. I was expecting you. Iboya and Piri, right?" Froken Snyder extended her hand to each of us with a friendly smile of welcome. After a brief evaluation of our comprehension in reading and writing, she gave Iboya and me books and asked us to write a composition for homework. I thought I would write about my new surroundings.

Early the next morning the warm rays of the sun shining in my eyes woke me up. On a clear day, the first thing I saw was the sun rising over the snow-covered landscape. After stretching for a few minutes, I climbed out of bed and seated myself at our writing table. The sun cast dancing spots on my open composition book and warmed my shivering slip-clad body.

I pretended to *be* the sun, watching all the creatures of the universe below. I let my fantasy run free. Instead of signing my name, I drew a sun's face and let him be responsible for my imaginary world.

I handed the composition in on Friday. On Sunday afternoon, when I was lazily lying on my bed daydreaming about David, there was a knock on my window. Outside stood Froken Snyder, accompanied by Herr Weinberg. They motioned for me to join them.

I put on my coat and came outside. They asked me to go for a walk. I felt apprehensive and shy as they placed me between them and started walking. Froken Snyder came right to the point. "Piri, yours was the best composition in the class. What made you treat the sun as God?" So she knew that I had written the composition. "Have you read something that gave you the idea?"

They were both looking at me expectantly. I needed time to answer, not wanting to be embarrassed, as I had been in Herr Weinberg's class. I looked down at our footprints, theirs deep-cut and edged, mine squashed and shapeless. I could distinguish the individual sounds our boots made in the hard snow; theirs was a heavy crunch from leather soles, mine a soft shuffle from rubber snowshoes. I felt sorry for ever having written the darn composition.

"Because I can feel his presence." The words came out involuntarily, but I felt that I had to explain. "Like now, I can feel his rays penetrate the cold, I can also see him."

"Very good, Piri. The sun is a tangible force," said Herr Weinberg, his eyes dancing.

"Don't you feel God's presence?" cut in Froken Snyder.

"My grandmother was a very pious woman," I said, not answering the question. "She had a close personal relationship with God. She could see Him and feel Him in everything she did."

"Were you raised by your grandmother?" Froken Snyder's voice was troubled.

"No, but I spent a lot of time with her on her farm."

"You must have loved her very much."

I lifted my face to the sun. My eyes burned as I looked for Babi in the sky. I could sense her anger at me for not believing the way she did, and I felt guilty. I lowered my eyes and scanned the icy water that surrounded the island.

"I'm going to give you an A for your composition, Piri, and you have to promise to write some more about your feelings."

Before I could think of a proper response for Froken Snyder, Herr Weinberg hit her with a snowball and she took off to retaliate, hopping in the deep snow like a kangaroo.

I wrote many other compositions during that winter, but never again with the same freedom. I felt self-conscious about having been exposed, and guarded my fantasies. However, that first composition earned me a high standing with Froken Snyder for the rest of my school stay.

On one of his early visits to our room to help Iboya and me with our science homework, David asked to see the "Sun" composition. He sat in a chair reading it, looking up at me from time to time, nodding his head in approval. After Iboya and I caught up to the rest of the class in science, he continued coming over, just to see me. I encouraged his visits in spite of Dora's warning.

"Hands off," she had said the first time she saw me talking with David after class. "He is Froken Apt's pet.

You don't want to be in trouble with the headmistress. You just barely got here. There are rules."

I could not imagine what Dora was talking about. Then I thought of the sexy black nightgown under the pillow. "But she's old enough to be his mother," I argued.

"She is not as old as she looks."

"Why isn't Herr Jonnson her lover? They are closer in age."

"But David is more her height; she does not even come up to the Giraffe's waist." Dora chuckled. "We call Herr Jonnson the Giraffe because he is so tall, and she is the Pekingese on account of her wobbly walk and round eyes." Dora turned serious for a moment. "Froken Apt came over here from Russia as a child; she is one of us. And she is completely devoted to us. A real softy in spite of her stern front. She has to maintain discipline; there are over a hundred of us against one of her."

The next time I saw David, I asked him about Froken Apt.

"She just tries to be my mother because she has no children and hasn't found a husband."

"But Dora told me . . ."

"Don't listen to her; you know how these Budapesti girls are. They have crazy ideas."

Whatever Froken Apt's motives were, she made it obvious that she was against our friendship. She always found an excuse to separate us. I suspected that she lectured David about wasting his time on a flirtatious relationship with me. In her presence he was always very careful to keep his distance from me. He would usually wait until after dusk to come by. He'd knock on my window, and depending on the weather, I would either go out and walk with him or invite him in.

It got simpler when spring came and we could sit out on the lawn, though even then I would imagine her eyes watching us from a remote window of the main house. The rest of the students had become accustomed to seeing us together and had stopped whispering. Dora no longer objected either; instead, she would join Iboya, David, and me on the grass, and together we would ponder what we would do after we became of working age and had to leave Visingso.

Since David, Iboya, and Dora were approaching eighteen, their departure was imminent. I hated the thought of being left behind, but when I told Iboya that I wanted to leave with her at the end of the summer, she protested adamantly.

"You stay and get some education. Look how much you have learned since we came here. If I have to leave, I'll come and visit you on weekends," she promised.

Pali kept writing all through the winter. In February Dora had asked me to send her regards to Hershi; she had had a crush on Hershi since they first met on the boat to Sweden. A week later, she received a letter from him, and they had been corresponding ever since. Pali and Hershi had been promising to come and visit us as soon as the island's cruise ship resumed its crossings. Sure enough, on the second Sunday in March, Dora and I were called to the main house, and there stood Pali and Hershi. I had mixed emotions as I greeted them. I did not like being hugged and kissed by Pali, but it gave us prestige to have visitors. Dora could not have been more delighted. She was beaming. Hershi acted quiet at first, but by the time we said goodbye at the boat, we were carrying on as if the four of us were old friends. After that first visit, they came almost every weekend, till I got sick of seeing Pali. When I finally refused to have Pali hanging around me, Iboya insisted that I stay as a fourth. "It will divert attention from you and David, and you'll serve as a chaperone for Dora," she explained.

Soon Hershi and Dora were falling in love, and they could no longer hide their feelings from onlookers. They held hands in public and talked about plans for their future. Since Dora had not found any family and she was an *einer allein,* one alone in the world, everyone was very happy for her. Hershi was trying to save money, so that when Dora was eighteen they could get married.

Pali was jealous, and angry with me for not being in love with him. He had found out about David and referred to him as "the junior scholar," which infuriated me. He also questioned Dora about our relationship.

"Don't mind him." Dora tried to calm me after one of Pali's visits. "He is just a very possessive person. He feels that because he has known you ever since you were a child, he has some sort of claim on you. Also, remember he lost all three of his sisters, as well as everyone else. You are his only link to home."

Now she had me feeling sorry for Pali.

"You know I don't dislike him; I just don't care for him romantically. He always has to make himself so important and conspicuous, like the time back home when he showed up with a flock of gypsy musicians under our window. You can't imagine how embarrassed I was in front of my mother and the rest of the family. Girls my age just did not get serenaded. Besides, there was a war on; my father was at the Russian front, and a serenade was the furthest thing from anybody's mind."

"What did your mother say?"

"She was amused by it. But then, you would have to have known my mother. She was not like anybody else's mother. Because she came from a small village where everybody was alike, she adored people who were daring. 'Avant-garde,' she called it. She would have loved you," I finished. It was not often that I let my mind wander to Mother.

Dora seldom talked about her parents, because they had separated before the war. She had lived with her mother and had seen her father only when she visited her grandparents in Miskolc. She remembered a very unhappy home from her early childhood. Her father was a professor and quite a flirt with the young women at the university. There were many bitter arguments that she overheard. Dora blamed it all on his looks. "He was too handsome and never seemed to age," she once told me, "even at forty when I last saw him before he was drafted into the army." Dora must have inherited his looks, with those large blue eyes and perfect features. Her thick brown hair by now had grown long enough to frame her face.

"Do you look like your father?" I asked, voicing my thoughts.

"Not my figure. It is short and dumpy," she said with distaste.

Actually, she was short, but certainly not heavy. "No, you are feminine, with your ample bosom and fine legs," I teased.

"It is my mother's body; I'll grow fat early if I don't watch it."

"What was your mother's face like?"

"She had dark eyes and dark hair, with milk-white skin." Dora paused. "When I last saw her in Auschwitz, her hair had been shaved off and she had lost so much weight her eyes looked like giant jet-black beads. The way she looked as we were being separated, that is how I remember her. I can't see her the way she used to be at home."

Suddenly I felt guilty for my wonderful memories of Mother.

Pali and Hershi came on a glorious Saturday toward the end of May. They brought food and we had a picnic. Pali produced a whole smoked eel from a paper sack for shock value, but it did not work. I had tasted it before and liked it. It was a popular food in Sweden. Even if I hadn't been introduced to it before, I would have eaten it anyway, just so he could not play big shot. After dessert, Pali and I went for a walk. He asked about "the junior scholar," and I told him, "He is going to be eighteen on June 6. He is exactly two years and four days older than I am."

"So does that mean he will be leaving school soon?" asked Pali, without hiding the glee on his sarcastic face.

I didn't give him the satisfaction of an answer. Instead, I looked him over. He was short, with a boy's physique and an old man's face. He had dark skin, a large nose, and dark eyes. His only two good features were brown wavy hair that he wore long and teeth so perfect that they looked false. He knew it and grinned a lot. His mouth was good, too, but the thought of kissing him made me ill. He tried on several occasions, but this time he was particularly persistent, so we had an argument.

After they left, Dora told me that Hershi had invited her to come to Stockholm for a visit during the school vacation. His aunt would write a letter to Froken Apt saying Dora could share a room with her daughter. I was happy for her, but jealous that she could spend all that time with Hershi. I wished I, too, could be off on a holiday, with David.

Then we had a halutz recruiter from Palestine come and visit the school. He tried to assure us that in spite of our displacement we all had a home there.

"You have to be patient," he said. "Your brothers and

sisters are fighting for your immigration. Right now the British are stopping all Jews from entering our homeland."

David interrupted by raising his hand and asking, "If Palestine is our homeland, why are the British in charge?"

The halutz massaged his forehead with the fingers of his right hand. "I'm glad you asked that. I'm used to the students in Palestine, where I'm a teacher. They crowd around radios, hang around in cafés and on street corners talking politics. To them it is a matter of life and death. But you come from a different experience. I should have remembered that . . . Forgive me." Clearing his throat, he asked, "You all know who Chaim Weizmann is?"

Some of us responded, "Yes." I was eager to be reminded of where I had heard the name before.

"In order to answer David's question, I will first have to tell you who this important man is. You should know about your own country's history. You must take pride in it." Straightening his shoulders, he went on: "Before emigrating to Palestine, Chaim Weizmann was a scientist in Great Britain. He discovered acetone, the ingredient used in the manufacture of explosives. It helped the Allies win the First World War. Because of this contribution, he was able to persuade the British to issue the Balfour Declaration. Are all of you familiar with this important event?" He surveyed the silent room, then continued: "It took place in 1917—Palestine was declared a Jewish homeland, and Britain was assigned to keep the peace between the Jews and the Arabs. It worked quite well, because at that time not too many Jews were heading for those shores, but now, with the aftermath of Hitler, Jews like yourselves with no other place to go are looking to Palestine as their only home. Because of this, the Arab neighbors are becoming inflamed, and have made a protest to stop Jewish immigration. The British disappointed us by giving in to Arab demands, and now the Jews are at war with the British and Chaim Weizmann feels deceived."

Another hand went up. "Is Chaim Weizmann an Englishman?" Good, I thought, I'm not the only one who is still confused.

The halutz looked out at us and shook his head understandingly. "Yes. Actually, he was born in Russia, and he's been the leader of the Zionists since Palestine was made a Jewish homeland." I remembered where I had heard his name before, along with Theodor Herzl's, who was the leader before him. It was at the Zionist meetings in Beregszász. They spoke of these two men as if they were sanctified. The halutz resumed his speech. "We shall win this war and thrust open the gates to all the Jews from the Diaspora, to come and rest their weary heads and never feel like outcasts again. We are finished with being refugees, turned out from all lands; we are building you a home!"

That evening, when David came to our room, we discussed with uncertainty the possibility of going to Palestine. Though the halutz talked feverishly about a place he considered the home of all Jews, we yearned to return to our old homes. We wanted the life we once had back, not the life he promised us. What we could not fathom was that after all that had happened to us nobody wanted to make amends or welcome us into our former countries. Even Palestine, the land of our biblical forefathers, was occupied by the British and closed to us. Still nobody cared. Nothing had made an impression. What makes us so undesirable, I asked myself.

Later, when David got up to leave, I walked out with him. We found the bench in the back of my bunk, and we sat very close. He put his arms around me and we kissed with a new passion. We needed to feel a sense of belonging. Holding on to each other, we did not speak.

The next day, when we met, we both felt shy and awkward.

The Palestinian man stayed on for a week. We sat around campfires and sang songs till we were hoarse. He told us about life on the kibbutz, how all the children were loved by and belonged to all the parents. Work was distributed among the members and responsibilities were shared by all. The profits from the kibbutz were used to better the country. Life was good because the people all had one goal. The halutz closed each of these gatherings by reassuring us, "When you are ready to emigrate, we'll have a place waiting for you, and you'll never have to fear losing it. You'll be home."

By the end of the week, many students had become devout Zionists, including David and two of his close buddies. Iboya remained neutral. "Don't commit yourself to anything," she warned me. She had been fervently trying to locate our American relatives through Jewish agencies, but we did not remember our aunts' married names or their addresses. The only thing Iboya remembered was Bridge-port as part of an address. We did not know if it meant city or state. Suri from Komjaty, who was still in the same refugee camp, had written in her last letter that she had found her relatives in America and that she was on the waiting list to emigrate there. She had promised to look for our relatives when she arrived.

Now that David had made up his mind to go to Palestine, I was torn in my loyalties. I knew that my place was with Iboya, but my relationship with David had gotten closer in the past week than it had been all winter, and I also felt a commitment to him.

A few days after her eighteenth birthday, Iboya was picked to go to work on a farm with the older girls. Froken Snyder as well as Herr Weinberg were going to be their chaperones. They were to be gone most of the summer. At last, Iboya and I could accept separation.

6

I became very friendly with my new roommate, Ida. She was actually Dora's roommate, but with Dora and Iboya gone, she moved in with me. Ida was a beautiful, introverted Polish girl between Dora's and my age, with an older sister who worked in a factory some distance from the school and visited only on holidays. She was in the same Swedish class with me. Both of us were quite fluent, and loved to leave the school grounds and meet Swedish teenagers. They found us fascinating, with our German experiences, and would invite us to their homes. I still found it hard to adjust to a family environment and only accepted on occasion, but Ida had become very close with one particular family on the island and spent a lot of time with them.

Browsing in the village one day, Ida and I stopped to look in the window of a sweetshop. Teenagers seated around tables were sipping coffee and munching pastries. Ida was yearning to go in. We each had some change in our pockets, but weren't sure if it would cover two coffees and a pastry to share. Timidly we entered and sat at a corner table. Ida asked to see a menu, and we realized our change would purchase only coffee. We sipped it very slowly so we could stay a long while. The kind waitress refilled our cups from time to time.

A blond, healthy-looking young woman carrying an armful of books joined her friends at the next table and declared in greeting, "I just can't wait to grow up so I can have a place of my own. I'll never be able to get all this work done at home." Her coffee arrived and she complained, "It is too weak."

"Aren't you going to have some pastry?" her friend offered.

"No, I'm getting too fat."

Ida and I exchanged glances, silently acknowledging the great difference between us and our Swedish peers. I felt a hopeless envy and wondered if we would always be outsiders or if our sense of values could change. Could we come to feel equal, not by imitating them, like Ida tried to do, but by coming to think like them?

Dora had written a couple of times, and from her letters I could tell she was not planning to return soon. She and Hershi were having a great time, and they were not about to part till she had to come back at the end of July. Even Froken Apt took a week off for a holiday, leaving Herr Jonnson in charge. With nobody to monitor us, David and I were together every evening. After classes he spent most of his time with his two friends, Orni and Dezso, kicking a soccer ball around. Herr Jonnson would join them on occasion.

Iboya wrote every week, telling me how much she loved the farm. It was a lot like Komjaty, she said. She described the fields of corn where she worked and the wild strawberry patch where she ate her fill, though the strawberries did not get as sweet as Babi's, she said. The wheat fields did not have poppies or bachelor buttons dotting them (not enough sun in this part of Sweden), but the farmers were very good people, and she loved being out of doors all day. In ending her letters she always gave me motherly warnings: "I hope you and David are not letting yourselves get into a situation you can't handle. Remember, we have a future in America, and he will be leaving soon for Palestine and a new life. You'll have plenty of time to fall in love." It was almost as if she had a crystal ball and could see that David and I were treading in dangerous waters.

The evening Froken Apt left for her holiday, David and I sat on our bench in back of my bunk and talked about our separate plans. Afraid of parting, we caressed each other. His hands moved toward my hair because he knew I loved the sensation of his fingers moving through the long strands. It was still a novelty, after having had all of it shaved off. Stroking my hair just naturally led to kissing, and soon David's body was trembling. It was both flattering and exciting to know that he desired me, but also very frightening. Signals went off in my head, and I brought everything to an abrupt stop. It was harder on David; his body was still aroused, and he could not turn it off at will. I said good night to him and went straight to bed. Ida was asleep in the upper bunk. I lay down on the lower bunk but could not fall asleep.

I wondered what Judi would say if she were watching, from wherever she was. She used to talk about wanting to make love to Gari. Would she really have been as brave if it had come down to it? If Gari had known, he would have found a way for them to make love, at least once, so Judi's wish would have come true. Now they would never know what it might have been like. David reminded me so much of Gari, they looked so similar. Sometimes when I was with him, I'd think he was Gari, and then I'd try to act as if I were Judi, the way she would handle a situation or answer a question. David would think I was imitating Dora. I wished Judi were there so I could talk things over with her.

I had tried not to think about Judi too often, because the memory of her put me into long depressions. I had difficulty recalling her face, the way it used to be before Germany. Instead, I would see her the way she looked on that first Sunday in Auschwitz, when I realized that she did not want to survive. The two of us were crying to see our mothers as we had been promised on our arrival by a woman with a megaphone. The blockova of our barrack came over to us: "You want your mothers? I'll show you where your mothers are—see the flames rising from those smokestacks?" She pointed in the direction of the crematoriums. "And if you are going to be crybabies, that is where you'll wind up." I saw the flicker of decision in Judi's eyes that I had learned to recognize when I first knew her. As for me, I was mortified and hated the blockova for what she said, but it made me stop crying. Every day, Iboya and I tried to persuade Judi to volunteer for work with us, but she could not be moved. "What sense would it make for me to live," she told us, "when thousands are being gassed each day?" She even gave up her meager meals. One afternoon when we returned from work, she was gone.

Ida climbed off her bed and sat down on mine, patting me. "Why are you crying? Can I help?"

By now I was heaving, shaking the whole structure of the bunk beds. "I'm crying for Judi, for my mother and my father, for all of them, and for myself."

"Soon Iboya and Dora will be back; that will help." Ida tried to comfort me. She shivered and climbed into my bed, pulling the blanket over both of us. "Listen, I'm kind of scared, too; I will have to leave here soon, and I have not told you, but my sister is . . . was . . ."

Ida could not get the words out. She swallowed and tried again. "My sister is planning to marry a Swedish man who is about to be discharged from his military service. They will be living with his family for a while, and where does that leave me? I wish I, too, could somehow blend in with the Swedes like a chameleon. I hate being who I am, an orphan, never able to go home, always dependent on strangers. They are looking to place me right now—in some factory with other lost souls. I don't mean to complain; it is nice of them to care and bother, they are the only ones who do, but I don't exactly look forward to leaving, now that I have made some friends." She snuggled up, I stroked her hair, and we fell asleep.

The next day, after our Swedish lessons, Ida and I went for a walk. On the way I told her about David and me petting last night. Ida in her frank manner commented, "You two better cool it." After we got home, I waited for David, but he did not come. I felt lonely and confused about his not showing up, and spent a restless night.

In the morning mail I received a homemade card of congratulations with some pressed wildflowers and a four-leaf clover from Iboya. It was my sixteenth birthday. I was supposed to be happy—it was a day I had thought about and wished for since I was a little girl—so why wasn't I? I remembered Iboya's sixteenth birthday in the ghetto—we did not have a party or a birthday cake, just half a roll each, but we still had Mother, Sandor, Joli, and the Gerbers.

David came and knocked on my window after supper. For a moment I stood undecided. Ida pushed me. "Go out and meet him; he might feel embarrassed about the other night." As soon as David saw me, he grabbed my hand and led me to the bench in the rear.

He had a small package and put it between us as we sat down. I opened it and saw inside a very pretty white comb with a handle. "Go ahead and try it," he urged. But

I reached for the card. It was a poem written on large-size construction paper, edged in artwork of tiny, lacy flowers; he must have labored over it for hours. The first verse was about my hair. The second spoke of two young lovers parting when their love has just started to bud and summer still holds flowers. I was convinced that his poem was a tragic expression of love second only to *Romeo and Juliet*, since they were condemned to die. I tried to act more sophisticated than my sixteen years, but when I looked up and saw his handsome face, the familiar forehead in deep furrows, my tears were unleashed, washing away the aloof, grown-up manner I had hoped to conduct myself in.

"You like it?" he asked.

"I do. It is the most beautiful poem I have ever read." David moved the gift and card to the side and pulled me close to him. When my wet cheek touched his, my love overwhelmed me. He whispered, "Happy birthday." We stayed out way past dark, and kissed in "adult fashion," as Judi used to say.

"Don't worry," David assured me, "I won't touch you the way I did last time." And he kept his promise.

Froken Apt returned from her holiday with her family in Stockholm, snapping us out of our leisure. The air was calm under summer skies, but there was an undercurrent that set us all on guard. She brought with her three passports—for David, Orni, and Dezso. The next day she took them shopping for clothing and luggage, got their hair cut, and by the time they returned at nightfall wearing identical beige belted raincoats, gray trousers, and brown loafers, they looked like three secret agents.

David showed up late that evening, just as Ida and I were preparing for bed. He talked with nervous excitement about his emigration to Palestine. "They need men desperately, and I am not doing anything important here. I don't know where I'll fit in, but as long as I can help and be part of building a new homeland for all the dispersed Jews, it will be worth the danger."

"What danger are you talking about?" I asked.

"The resistance fight with the British. We probably will be smuggled in on a cargo ship from Marseilles."

"But I thought you had a passport."

"That is just to take us to France. We can't get entry into Palestine because, as the halutz said, it is occupied by the English and they have halted all immigration. I'll probably join one of the partisan groups like the Irgun when I get there. Without military training, I can't join the army."

I looked at David, barely a man, and reflected on Henri and Gari in the Underground, and the young Ukrainian soldiers' bodies I had once seen floating in the Rika. I thought, boys enter manhood just in time for another war. What is the purpose of their lives—to fight an endless battle? They kiss us goodbye and go off to die. What good is falling in love?

"So you survived the camps just to go off and be killed fighting the British? It doesn't make sense."

"There is always a risk, but if we win, there will be a Jewish homeland. We won't have to live in fear of being turned out again with nowhere to go," David explained. "Maybe you and Iboya will change your minds and come to settle there."

"Now you sound like the halutz, but if you had listened closely, you would have also heard him say that Palestine is surrounded by hostile Arabs whose main objective in life is to kill Jews. So if you succeed in driving out the British, you'll just be fighting an older war."

At this point Ida, who had been quiet during our discussion, chimed in with her history-book statistics. "Sweden managed to stay out of war for a hundred and forty years. They are a people of tolerance and understanding, without greed or hostility; they take care of their poor and their sick. It is the only real socialized country. We have had enough of war and persecution." She paused, then came to the point. "The Swedes are generous to invite us to stay and become Swedish citizens, so why not grab our chance for a safe future?"

"Because we will still be living in a Christian society," David answered. "Besides, we cannot think only of ourselves; what about all the other thousands of homeless Jews—the rest of the survivors still in refugee camps in Germany, the Jews in Russia and all the other countries where they live in fear? No, the only solution to our dilemma is a Jewish homeland, or we'll be at the mercy of another anti-Semitic uprising, another Hitler."

David not only had a new haircut and new clothes, he was also charged by a new purpose. I was afraid for him, yet in some envious way admired him. He had a sense of himself, a commitment that would fill the empty spaces left by the lost members of his family. Looking at him, I could already see anticipation taking charge. He stood taller, more confident, and eagerness lit up his black eyes.

When I walked him outside to say good night, David embraced me and practically crushed my ribs. His lips were forceful, his body hard and imposing. I felt overpowered—not an unpleasant sensation, but threatening. After a few seconds, I struggled free of his hug, but the imprint of his muscular physique lingered.

He leaned against the wall. "Do you care for me enough to follow, after it is safe? I know we are young in years, but we are old by experience. We have to make our own decisions; we are nobody's children." I could feel his gaze piercing through the dark of the evening. "I know Iboya wants to take you to America, but in the end, it is really up to you. I would like to know how you feel before I leave."

We had never talked seriously about us. I was taken aback and unprepared. I also felt unsure of his sincerity, as if I was being tested. When I spoke, the words came in a stutter. "We are still looking for some family, somebody still might turn up. My father might have survived the Russian prison camp, and not know how to find us. Perhaps your father is alive, too. You don't know; we have to keep looking through those lists of survivors."

I was also thinking of Henri, my first boyfriend. What if he was alive—who would I choose?

David said, "I would just like to know if I'm leaving anyone behind, or if I stand alone. Is there a commitment between us, or don't I mean anything to you?"

I was on the verge of tears. "I care for you very much of course, but everything is so uncertain. I don't even know where I'll be next month; if Iboya has to leave here, I want to go with her."

Suddenly he became compassionate. "Never mind, you don't have to answer now; I'll write as soon as I can. But promise you will think about it, and will answer my letters with honesty."

Ida sat up in her bed as I came in. She scanned my confused face. "Do you want to talk about it?" she offered.

"He asked if I would follow him to Palestine."

Her eyes showed surprise. "I guessed he was serious, but not to that extent. Did he say that he was in love with you?"

"No."

"Well, don't worry about it; it could be fear of leaving.

He tries to convince himself that he has made the right choice, but he is scared to be alone again, to make another start in a new country with strange people. Sure they are Jews, but they speak a different language and they don't share his experiences."

"He said he will write, and I should think about my answer."

"Once he gets to Palestine, he will be too preoccupied to think of love, and if you are smart, you better start planning what you and Iboya will do with your lives. This school is just a temporary stop."

Ida's words sounded harsh, almost sinister. Perhaps she is jealous, I thought, convinced that David would not forget me.

Froken Apt made an announcement at the following Friday's supper. "Tomorrow evening we are going to have a farewell party in honor of David, Dezso, and Orni's departure to Palestine, and you are all invited for refreshments." Everyone burst into an enthusiastic round of applause, but my hands were silent. I looked over at David's table and felt hurt, seeing his joyous, sportive mood as his friends joked with him and the two others. I would have liked to run from the dining room, but I sensed several students' and Froken Apt's observant eyes on me.

Ida and I did leave right after dessert. It was still early, and Ida suggested we go for a walk. We wound up at her Swedish family's house, where we were warmly welcomed and I was distracted from being irritable. By the time we returned at dusk, finding our school restored to its normal pace, I was calmed down. We settled in our room, reading Swedish novels lent to us by Ida's family.

At the party the following night, there were trays of cookies and a hundred bottles of Pommac, Swedish soda pop—a rare treat—donated for the occasion by one of the merchants on the island. The boys stood around the ping-pong table toward the left wall of the entrance. The girls, with freshly shampooed hair and wearing their best skirts and blouses, took the liberty of clustering around the three young men being honored.

Froken Apt, in a lightweight navy dress with white organza collar and cuffs, her cherubic face animated, walked among us waving her lace handkerchief. She caught me watching her, and the lace handkerchief stopped in midair just a few inches from me. It had the same flowery fragrance I had smelled in her room when she let Iboya and me take a rest there on our arrival.

"You must have a good time, Piri," she whispered, a glimmer of sadness softening her face. "Come, let's have a fresh bottle of Pommac." I followed her suspiciously toward the table. "What have you been hearing from your friend Dora?" she asked. "Is she planning to marry the redheaded young man?"

"I don't know," I said noncommittally.

"She is too young. You are just children, all of you. You need to grow and learn. I wish we could keep you here till you are . . ." Froken Apt gave me a concerned look, almost maternal. "How is your health these days?"

"I'm well, thank you." The words came out defensively. I did not like discussing or reflecting on my health. I'd had too many sick days at school. Froken Apt took the clue and changed the subject.

Our conversation was suddenly drowned out as the students burst into an impromptu medley of Hebrew songs we had learned during the halutz's visit. Within minutes, dance circles formed and Froken Apt and I were pulled into them. The walls and wooden floors became amplifiers, resounding to our energetic tempo. The best thing about dancing the hora was the way the linking of arms, the synchronizing of feet, and the harmonizing of voices joined us in a common spirit—not only in celebration, but in offering our support for the three scouts' safe journey to Palestine. We sang and danced till our bodies were soaked with perspiration, our voices exhausted, and all the bottles of Pommac emptied. After thanking Froken Apt for the party, we walked to our quarters with hope in our hearts.

Ida, David, and I walked off together. Ida paused at our door and said, "Well, I guess this is really goodbye," as she extended her hand to David. "I wish you everything you wish yourself. Do a good job, and who knows, maybe if things don't work out for me in Sweden, we might meet again."

David kissed her on the cheek. "Shalom, Ida, I hope it will work for you."

Ida went into the room. David and I walked to our bench and sat down. "The sky is crowded with stars," I said.

"We are leaving early tomorrow. I might not see you in the morning," he whispered, stroking my hair and stilling my voice with a kiss. I heard the noisy crickets and felt a gentle summer breeze brush over us.

"Orni and Dezso are waiting up for me, I can't stay long. We have some last-minute details to go over."

The spell was broken. My romantic mood turned to anger, which I covered up with indifference. "It doesn't matter. I'm exhausted anyway and we have school tomorrow."

David's thick eyebrows went up, as if I were the one who had said something wrong. Men are so dumb sometimes, I thought, as we walked to my door.

"Piri, do you remember what I asked you the other night? You must think about us and let me know in your first letter what you decide. It will make a big difference to me, in what choice I'll make when I get to Palestine. Do you understand what I'm asking of you, Piri?"

I was not certain, but he looked so serious that I was touched, and promised to think about it.

His parting kiss was long. Then he let go, raising his hand in a wave, smiling as he faded into the shadows of the night.

Iboya and her group returned at the end of August, just in time to snap me out of my longing for David. He had been gone over a week. Iboya looked better than I had ever remembered seeing her, her skin tanned and her hair sun-bleached in platinum streaks. She looked healthy and full of vitality, as beautiful as she used to be before the war. As a matter of fact, the whole group looked revitalized. The fresh air and hard work seemed to have chased away the ghosts from their recent past and given them back their youth.

Iboya and I talked late into the night. She told me about the marvelous mare at the farm which she got to ride almost every evening. "From the first time I mounted her, we were friends. She was the only one who could be ridden without a saddle, and since I can only ride bareback, we were compatible. I just let her travel the path at her own pace, a slow, proud trot. It was flat farmland as far as I could see, divided into neat fields of beans, wheat, and potatoes. I loved looking down from on top of the horse, seeing the countryside stretched out around me. The houses were set close to the road, and riding by, I could look into some of the windows and see families sitting around their supper tables . . . not too different from the farmers in Komjaty. I guess people are the same everywhere."

"Someone should have told that to Hitler," I said.

"That is another thing about the country; out in the

open fields I looked at things differently. I felt fortunate and grateful that at least two of us survived and that we have each other. Now it is up to us to do something worthwhile with our lives, something to count for having been spared. Do you follow what I'm trying to say?"

"I'm not sure," I answered. "Have you accepted the fact that we are alone and no one else has been saved?"

"I have not given up hope," Iboya said. "I'm still praying for the possibility, but we have to be realistic, too. The war has been over more than a year and the lists are passed around and posted everywhere; our names are on all of them . . ."

The loneliness I tried to keep at a distance suddenly enveloped me. With all the talk about new beginnings in America, Palestine, and Sweden, deep within me I still held fast to the conviction that I'd be going home. But now my secret dream of traveling the road back to Hungary and picking up my former life was shattered. Iboya's voice trailed off and in the silence I felt a chill that covered my skin with goose bumps.

I remembered our last day in Auschwitz when, during the selection, Iboya was picked as part of a transport to go to Christianstadt and I was left back with the discards —the weak and the sick no longer fit for work. At the last minute, as the transport was moving toward the bathhouse, we spotted Mrs. Berger, a friend of mother's from Beregszász, who was returning from her work as a sorter of clothing. This was a very privileged work detail—she wore a white kerchief to set herself apart. Sometimes she found food among the belongings of the new arrivals and would share it with us, as on this occasion.

Secretly passing a small parcel to Iboya in the moving line, she asked why Iboya was crying.

"We have been separated; Piri is over there." Iboya pointed to where I stood crying convulsively.

Mrs. Berger looked around and, in the flash of a second, managed a miracle. With one hand, she pulled a crying mother out of the transport and deposited her back with her daughter, while with her other hand, she swung me over into the moving line. I slowly worked my way up toward Iboya as inconspicuously as possible, controlling my relief and joy at being reunited. Even when I was finally alongside her, trying to keep up the pace five abreast, I only communicated silently with my puffy eyes.

Not till the lines were halted outside the bathhouse, to wash away the soot of Auschwitz before our departure, did we dare to speak. Iboya reached out and took my hand. "We are leaving this godforsaken place together." Guiding me to the rear, away from the crowd, Iboya eased us to the ground, untying the bundle Mrs. Berger had given her. It contained a large chunk of stale bread, some spoiled pastries, and a small piece of mildewed cheese. Iboya proceeded to divide it up. I reached for the pastry. It was the first sweet I had eaten in Auschwitz. In spite of its rancid taste, I devoured it in two bites and licked my dirty fingers.

"Are you sleeping?" Iboya called up to me, interrupting my reminiscence.

"No," I answered. "I was thinking that we almost did not have each other. If Mrs. Berger hadn't happened to come by at that moment . . ."

"I've thought of her, too, many times," said Iboya, her voice low. "That is just what I am trying to say, Piri. Mrs. Berger's presence was more than chance. She was sent by someone to spare you."

"You mean like God, or Babi?"

"She did not know our Babi, I mean like Mother. You know Mother didn't have a choice, she had to go with the little ones, but she watches over us. I really believe that."

I choked up at the mention of Mother. I could not get my mind away from Auschwitz. I could see Mother so clearly there, in the bright sunlight. She got out of the cattle car first. Then Iboya handed down Sandor and Joli before jumping down herself. Everyone had gotten out, but I was still standing at the ledge, looking outward, wondering what kind of factory they had brought us to.

Mother's face was exhausted as she looked up at me. "Piri, jump," she called. Her voice was anguished and panic-stricken. It was a big drop. She stretched her arms up to catch me. There were hundreds of people around us, pushing and shoving, not knowing which way to go. Children were crying to be picked up, scared of being trampled.

Male prisoners tried to organize us. One came over and, speaking in Yiddish, asked how old I was. "Thirteen," I said.

"*Nein, nein!*" he said, "*Du bist sechzehn.*" Turning to Iboya, he repeated the question. When she said she was sixteen, he told her to say she was seventeen, and rushed over to some other teenagers. We looked to Mother for an explanation. "He must have a reason for saying it, and he is one of us, so you better listen to him."

A woman with a shrill voice was shouting orders through a megaphone in Hungarian with a German accent: "Men to the right—women and children to the left; keep the lines moving." The five of us stayed together. "Don't be alarmed. This is a temporary separation. You will be reunited on Sunday."

I walked along bewildered, not noticing that the lines in front of us were being divided, till we faced four SS men. One of them held an officer's baton. Another asked Iboya and me our age. We replied as we had been warned. The one with the baton extended his arm like a fencer's and let it fall between Mother and the two little ones, pushing them away from her. Mother stood petrified while seconds passed. Then, leaving us, she rushed to pick up Joli and took Sandor by the hand. "They need me more," she told the hostile and annoyed SS man with the stick. Turning to us, her eyes murky, she said, "Be brave and look after each other." It was her last act as our mother, setting an example to last us a lifetime.

"I miss Mother so much," I sobbed into my pillow.

"Now you're crying," Iboya said. "That won't help anything."

"And what about Father in Russia? He could be alive! Rozsi, Etu, Lilli, and her family—they can't all be dead."

"Piri, I have been going over each possibility. Mother, Sandor, and Joli perished on the day of our arrival at Auschwitz. Father, if he endured the prison camp, knows what took place and would not expect any of us to come back. If he made contact with his brother Sruel in Russia, he might have stayed there and started a new life. Lilli, Lajos, and Manci could not have survived the massacre in Poland, not from the stories we heard. Besides, if Lilli was alive, she of all the others would have gone home. Rozsi, we heard two conflicting stories about. If she was picked for a transport right after they arrived in Auschwitz, as the Smilovitz girls said, and lived, by now we would have seen her name on one of the lists."

"So you think they were just sparing our feelings?" I asked.

"I tend to believe Frida's story that she went with Babi to the left. You know how devoted she was to her. That brings us to Etu, and I have speculated a lot about her . . ."

"But I remember Shafar told Mother that he had not seen her for some time before he left Budapest, and thought that her Christian friends might have gotten her false papers," I said.

"On the other hand, he also told me that a lot of cattle cars had been filled with Jews from Budapest by the time he came to our ghetto. They were rounding up people on the streets, checking their papers, night and day." Iboya's voice grew heavy. She yawned and soon dozed off. I tried to shut my eyes and still my mind, but I was too stirred up. In the dark and quiet room, I gathered the family members together again and seated them around our large kitchen table. If only I could see them like that one more time, as in the past, when I would return from a summer holiday in Komjaty, always anxious that nothing at home had changed in my absence. They would all be there to greet me, talking and asking questions, and the kitchen would be filled to overflowing with merriment.

But I had been away from home more than two years, and not on a summer holiday. The kitchen I was dreaming of was a long distance from Sweden, and I told myself that Iboya was right; I couldn't shut my eyes on all that had taken place.

I spent a restless night interrupted by a repeating nightmare. I was back in the congested cattle car, separated from Mother; I tried to push through the crowds of people, but the faceless bodies kept multiplying, dividing us more and more, till I lost sight of her. My own sobbing awakened me. Lying in my bunk bed surrounded by darkness, I tried to figure out where I was, to sort out reality from the dream. Neither seemed acceptable. I longed for my brass bed at home. Afraid to continue the dream, I forced my eyes open and stared out my little window, waiting for my friend the sun.

Dora arrived the next day, wearing the look of Stockholm. I felt out of sorts, almost irritated by her well-being. She told me in detail about her "intimate relationship" with Hershi. Realizing my shock, she concluded, "We are going to be married as soon as he can afford to get his own apartment. With both of us working, we'll manage the rest."

She gave me a letter from Pali, which I waited to read till I was alone. I had to laugh out loud when I read his invitation to come visit him in Stockholm. I would have liked to see Stockholm and visit all the marvelous places Dora wrote me about, had the invitation been extended by David.

Pali also promised to take me to the theater in Stockholm, describing the evening the three of them went together. The only theater I had seen was the one we set up in our back yard. We would put boards across bricks for benches, rig up old cartons for a stage, and charge five filler for sitting and three for standing. I had never been inside a real theater. It sounded so exciting, but Pali's company was too high a price. Besides, Iboya would never permit me to go.

I spent the rest of the weekend listening to Dora; our friendship picked up where we had left off. I realized that my anxiety was not her fault. I was missing David.

The Monday after Dora's return, as Iboya and I came into the dining room for lunch, Froken Apt called us aside and handed Iboya a telegram from France. While she tore it open, I closed my eyes and prayed. I felt Froken Apt put her arm around me. Then Iboya's voice split the waiting hush in the room. I had to make her repeat what she said before I dared accept it. "Etu is alive! Our sister Etu is alive!" Soon we were surrounded, the tables of food abandoned. Iboya and I embraced. Everybody wanted to touch the telegram. When it came to me, I read the printed words over and over: STAY

WHERE YOU ARE, LETTER TO FOLLOW. I felt a rekindling of hope that others in our family might also be alive, but I kept it to myself.

Iboya and I speculated for ten days about what Etu might be doing in Marseilles, France. Then I received my first letter from David, telling me how he, Orni, and Dezso had gone to the Palestine Bureau and were talking in Hungarian when this woman sitting in the waiting room jumped out of her chair and came over to them, explaining breathlessly that she had been stopping in for several days, hoping to find some of her family. She said she was looking for two sisters just around their age named Piri and Iboya Davidowitz.

"When I told her that we had just left you in Sweden," the letter continued, "your poor sister broke down; she laughed and cried all at once, hugging and kissing me; then she took my hand and walked me to the telegraph office so I could write the address correctly on the telegram. I can just imagine the happiness you and Iboya experienced on receiving the news. I wish I could have been there to see you. I miss you very much. I don't know how long we'll have to wait for a boat to Palestine, but they promised to give us preferential treatment because of our military status. As for your sister, it might be a long wait, but she is very determined."

Some of our questions about Etu were answered. I also read "I miss you very much," over and over. And the letter was signed, "With much love." I was not sure that David would still be in Marseilles when my letter got there, but I sat down and wrote back the same day. I did not answer his question about us, because I was still uncertain.

Etu's letter arrived ten days after her telegram. Iboya read it out loud.

Etu said she was married to a man named Geza Weisfried:

We went home after the war ended, and waited, hoping that somebody would show up to witness our marriage, but the only relation that returned was our cousin Nathan Mermelstein. His wife and two children had perished in Auschwitz. He was trying desperately to find a way out of Communist Hungary, to emigrate to America, to join his parents, sisters, and brothers. Before he left Beregszász, Geza and I got married. What I'm about to tell you, as to how we found our house, will make you cry. I'm only doing it in case you might be thinking about returning there. Don't. It is no longer our house. We found a Christian family living in it. With great difficulty, they finally agreed to let Geza and me stay in one room. But they were suspicious and resentful, making us feel very uncomfortable. I had to fight with them for a chance to let me use the stove. Anyway, the house was torn apart, in shambles. All the inside doors were missing, used for firewood. We had to hang up a sheet for some privacy. The neighbors acted strange and unfriendly. I had to explain to them who I was; they did not recognize me. I know I had been in Budapest for the last couple of years, but I was born in that house. I kept thinking of Mother, how friendly she was with all of them. I felt rejected and hurt. Even Mrs. Molnar next door hardly took the time to hear me out when I went over with Geza to ask for her assistance in explaining to the strangers that it was our house. "You've changed so," she said, barely looking up at me. "Everything has changed here, too," she went on, complaining about the hardships they had suffered during the German occupation, and now with the Russian takeover.

"But at least you were allowed to stay together in your own homes and you are all alive. I'm alone," I cried.

Her daughter Ica (Piri's friend) came up to me with

apologies for her mother's behavior. "She has not been well since the war. But you are *not* alone. Iboya and Piri wrote twice from Germany, telling us that they got good treatment and would be coming home after the war."

"They changed their minds no doubt," Mrs. Molnar cut in. "Why come back here to poverty. We heard that a lot of the Jews have gone on to America and have gotten rich."

Ica has grown into a beautiful young woman, the only friendly face I encountered. She followed us back to our house to explain to the people. Later she brought me the two postcards. I told her that I knew all about those cards, how the Germans made you write them for the world to think you were well treated. Ica seemed confused and said, "Well, anyway, I could not answer them, there was no return address." I'm sorry but I had to tell her the address was Auschwitz. Piri's poor little innocent friend was horrified and could only say, "I also took good care of Piri's gramophone."

Your last postcard was postmarked July 1944. I have spoken to some of the people who came back, so I was aware of what took place on your arrival in Auschwitz. Still, I kept hoping. It was impossible to believe those monstrous stories, so Geza and I went on living in that room for a while. He got a job, I got pregnant. Then I had a miscarriage and lost the baby. It was foolish for us to think that we could build new lives on top of smoldering ashes. Geza wanted to leave right away, but I kept thinking stubbornly that somebody would return. Not till winter was approaching, and I was afraid of not being able to cross the borders in the snow, did I finally give in to Geza's pleading. I couldn't trust anybody to tell them that we were leaving the country except Ica Molnar. She asked me to tell Piri that she is sorry. In the end I was glad to leave the house. The memories and nightmares were driving me insane, especially when I saw the sandbox and the strange children playing in it. There was a little boy from across the street who kept coming over and asking if Sandor had returned yet. Why am I going on like this? Forgive me.

When Geza and I emigrate to Palestine, we'll build a home there and you will come and join us. This young man, David, told me that you are trying to get in touch with our relatives in America. That would be very sensible. It would give Geza and me a chance to get settled and by then the political situation maybe will have improved.

You are probably wondering who Geza is. He is from Budapest. We met in a work camp, where he helped me secure some food and winter clothing during the war. He is twenty-eight and an ardent Zionist. He left what remained of his family, a mother and sister, in Budapest, in hopes of having them follow us when immigration to Palestine opens up. We are not sure what is awaiting us there, but we don't want to live in Hungary with the Russians. We want to help in building a Jewish homeland, to prevent a recurrence of our experiences. Otherwise we could never bring children into this world in good conscience.

I almost forgot to tell you that I found some pictures at the photographer's on Main Street. They are doing big business with returning Beregszászi like myself, knowing that we will pay any price for an old photograph of our loved ones. They are developing all their old negatives and displaying them in their show windows. Unfortunately, I could not find any of our parents, just one old group picture of Lilli, Lajos, Rozsi, myself, Piri, Sandor, and Manci. Also one of Lilli alone. The big oil portraits of Father and Mother hanging over the brass beds have vanished, along with all other things of value.

Etu asked that we write as soon as possible. She gave the address of the Palestine Bureau, explaining that in case they left Marseilles, letters would be forwarded to them in Palestine.

Finishing the letter, Iboya exclaimed, "Thank God, there are three of us."

"No, we are four. She has a husband."

In spite of so many things happening in the course of the summer, it came to an abrupt and disappointing end. All staff and students were called to an assembly where Froken Apt informed us that the school was breaking up. "Only a handful of children under eighteen remain, and it would not pay for us to lease the summer camp for another year."

Ida was invited to live with her Swedish family in Visingso. We were glad for her. Dora returned to Stockholm and Hershi with high hopes, while Iboya and I, through no choice of ours, were being sent to a factory in Varnamo.

We were given one week to prepare for our departure. I walked the grounds of the school and looked about me with sadness. Everything was familiar and meaningful. I sat on the old wooden bench and thought of David and the danger he might meet trying to enter Palestine illegally. In the late afternoons remaining, I walked to the shore and stared at the blue water. I said goodbye to the Visingso teenagers, the teachers, and Froken Apt. She gave me a hug, and I burst into tears.

The morning of our departure I gazed at the rising sun and wondered if I would ever feel its warmth from my new dwelling. Iboya, too, seemed restless and moody as we packed our few belongings, but she tried to hide it from me.

"We'll get used to our new place in no time, and you'll make new friends," she comforted me as we sailed away from Visingso with eight other girls just as apprehensive as Iboya and I.

We were put up in a small inn called the Vindruva, which had been converted into a crowded rooming house. Everybody here spoke Hungarian. Iboya and I had to share a room on the ground floor with a redheaded girl called Johana. There were over forty women living in the Vindruva, ranging in age from sixteen to forty-five. I was the youngest. A calendar was fixed on the hall wall, for kitchen detail. Apparently we had to take turns as kitchen helpers after our eight hours at the raincoat factory, where we were to start work Monday.

Iboya soon got accustomed to our new schedule, but my energy would run out in midafternoon. I often got into bed as soon as we arrived home from the factory at 5:30 P.M. I had to stand on my feet all day, by a long workbench. There would be tall stacks of raincoat collars waiting for me every morning. The woman at the bench in front of mine would fold over and double the pattern given to her by the cutter, then glue them on the wrong side. My job was to run a small roller over each collar to get out the bubbles, then turn it right side out and roll it again on the outer edges so it would lie perfectly smooth when it was sewn onto the coat. After I became more skillful, I was allowed to work on sleeves and belts, rolling the glued seams and turning them right side out.

Some of the women were saving out of their meager pay to purchase a sample of our own handiwork. The raincoats were considered quite chic, the Sherlock Holmes type, and were exported to many countries, even the United States. But my raincoat money was spent in a sweetshop. This confection-perfumed heaven had a round bittersweet-chocolate ball rolled in chocolate sprinkles, with a rum-flavored soft center, one bite of which was worth a whole raincoat. We called it *monyos.* On Saturday afternoons, the women who had acquired these raincoats would take orders from the rest of us for *monyos* and Napoleon pastry, a favorite with Hungarians, who claimed its origin, and get all decked out to go strolling on Main Street. This way, carrying the white pastry boxes, they could have a legitimate reason for looking over the boys of Varnamo and being seen by them.

I'm sure the *monyos* had nothing to do with it—I could never afford enough of them to make me sick—but as soon as winter approached, I developed a fever and spent many weeks in the hospital. Iboya visited me every day, and most of the Vindruva tenants stopped in from time to time. The doctors were so awed and fascinated by my experiences that they took turns examining me, not believing that there was nothing more wrong than my heart murmur and digestive difficulties. One doctor, who did not give me any physical exams, asked me many questions, about both my childhood and the Germany experiences. I was not aware of it at the time, but looking back, I realized he was a psychiatrist.

The worst of winter was over by the time I was released, and Iboya informed me that the Vindruva was closing down and we would be moving to Jonkoping, where we would be working in a match factory. As much as I hated to be uprooted again, I was not sorry to leave the raincoat factory with its constant fumes of rubber and glue.

What was so strange about our Swedish travels thus far was that we had remained basically within the same region: the southern triangle, with Malmö at the point, hugging the shore of the Kattegat. Jonkoping is inland, snuggled between Huskvarna, where the famous motorcycles are made, and Göteborg, the second largest city in Sweden.

The train ride from Varnamo to Jonkoping took less than an hour. Our group of fourteen was met by a social worker, who accompanied us to our new apartment house on Västra Storgatan, the main street. We walked into a huge courtyard of cobblestones. I had the feeling of being closed off in a large vault, with the heavy gates forming the fourth wall. Iboya and I were put in a room on the first floor of a two-story complex in the rear. Our large window faced into the courtyard, from where we could see people going in and out of the side buildings, and if the iron gates were left ajar, we could glimpse the street. Our room had minimal furniture—two beds, a chest of drawers, two chairs, and a small square table. We had no kitchen. A hot noonday meal would be available for a reasonable price in the factory's cafeteria, and weekend and other meals would become our own responsibility. Down the hall there were a couple of hot plates for communal use.

After showing our group around the buildings and putting our names on the mailbox, the social worker took us through the marketplace and introduced us to some of the shopkeepers. She stayed with our group for the rest of the day, leaving her phone number, in case of any emergency. Iboya copied it down carefully into her address book and inquired about a doctor, "in case Piri gets sick." Giving me a reassuring smile that was not too convincing, the social worker said, "Oh, she will be well from now on, but I will paste the number and address of a doctor you could call on the hall telephone."

She left us and we closed the door on our small room, feeling forsaken, totally on our own in a strange city. We could hear the sounds of the other tenants in the building as they went about their chores. When we had passed some of them in the hallway earlier, the social worker introduced us and asked them to show us to the gates of the match factory on Monday morning. They looked our group up and down, to see if we would fit in. Iboya and I in turn searched their faces, hoping to recognize one of them, since they were also refugees, but they were strangers, mostly from Poland. For the first time since the camps, we were left on our own, and it was frightening.

I walked over to Iboya, who was looking out on the dusk of the courtyard, and asked if she thought we could manage.

"We will have to be very careful with our money. The reason I bought only milk, bread, and butter at the market is that I want to see if we can budget for fruits and vegetables after we know how much our wages will allow. Meat looked very expensive, too, but if we eat our main meal at the factory and it's sufficient, then we won't cook."

"Anyway," I said, "we have no dishes or anything for housekeeping."

"We'll do the best we can, Piri. After all, we can't be dependent on the Swedes forever. They have certainly given us a good start and Suri's papers are almost ready for emigration to America, according to her last letter. I have faith in her finding our relatives."

Iboya and I had one of those nights when we reminisced about too many things till we were wide awake. We got hungry, ate most of our bread and butter, and finally fell asleep as it was getting light.

Midmorning, we were awakened by someone knocking on our door. I sat up in alarm and looked at Iboya. "We don't know anyone here," she said, puzzled and suspicious. "It is Sunday morning, isn't it?" She walked to the door and asked, "Who is it?"

"You won't believe it, open up and see." The voice had a familiar, teasing squeak. Turning to me for assurance, Iboya unlocked the door, with her body concealed and her head poking out. The door was pushed open and Magda Hollander burst in, with arms wide to embrace Iboya. They hugged, jumped around, and both spoke at the same time, blending the words into gibberish. I could not take my eyes off Magda during their greeting. Her delicate heart-shaped face had a pink blush, her almond-shaped brown eyes held a mischievous light, and her small narrow lips were like a kitten's. Magda's body had filled out, her bosom overly abundant for her five-foot two-inch frame and thin limbs, a Hollander family characteristic. In my mind's eye I saw her emaciated, her eyes all but lost in their sockets and underlying puffs, cheekbones protruding, her large breasts empty like deflated casings, bundled in rags, her wooden clogs stuffed with paper and straw to warm and cushion her swollen ankles as she shuffled to keep up with the lines during our death march. Only her mother's urging to carry on for another mile, another day, kept her going. Her feet, like a robot's, dragged along to Mrs. Hollander's persistent cry, "Keep moving for my sake, because if you stop, you'll take all three of us down with you." What pleasure Mrs. Hollander would derive if she could see her daughter now. Again, I found myself hoping Babi's belief was true, that the dead are able to observe the living.

Finally Magda bent over and hugged me, sitting on my bed. We took turns asking each other questions, in order to catch up on lost time. "Elza is married to a Swedish man. He is one of those you see all over Sweden wearing a white school cap with a navy visor. He still has some six months of college left, so for the time being, Elza is living with her mother-in-law in Ryd. She earns her keep by dressmaking. They got her a sewing machine. I just came from there and stopped to pick up my mail, when I saw your name on the box."

"Where is your room?" I asked.

"Right across the hall," Magda said, throwing her arms around me in her exuberance.

"Is there anybody else here that we know?" Iboya asked, getting to her feet and starting to dress with purpose.

"No one from Christianstadt, but Hajnal Friedman is here from Beregszász. You must know her. She has two younger sisters, Aranka and Lilli."

"Sure we know her," Iboya rushed to answer. "Are the other two alive also?"

"Yes, but they live in different cities. Hajnal probably went to see them and will be back in the evening. That's what we do on weekends. We all go visiting. The only reason I came back early is that I have a boyfriend and we have a date. I'll let you meet him when he brings me home. He is a survivor like us, working as a dairy inspector." Both Iboya and I started to snicker, our eyes focused on her bosom. Magda adjusted her brassiere straps with a grin of acknowledgment.

Magda called on us later in the evening. "Come to my room," she said. "My boyfriend brought milk and I picked up some pastries."

Iboya and I looked at her in surprised appreciation.

"Don't think that I've forgotten how kind the two of you were to my mother."

Günter was a pleasant-looking, chubby-faced man in his mid-twenties. He spoke Swedish with a German accent I found jarring. While we were conversing, there was a knock on the door and Magda went to open it.

Iboya gasped and jumped up. "My God, Hajnal Friedman." I got up, too, and waited for my turn to embrace her. She had aged terribly. Her family used to live on our street years ago, when she was a teenager. Now she looked like her own mother.

"Magda told me you would be here, and I just had to say hello." Hajnal was clutching a letter in her right hand. "I got this a while back from my girlfriend, Buzsi Kertes; she still lives on your street in Beregszász. Do you girls remember her? She has a son the same age as your brother Sandor."

"Of course, I knew Tomas," I said. "He used to come and play with Sandor and Manci in our sandbox before the separation of Christians and Jews. He was a bright boy." I recalled an incident when Tomas handed Sandor a wheel from a broken tricycle, saying, "You be the pilot and fly the airplane. I'll sit next to you and tell you which way to go, and we'll let Manci be a passenger." While Sandor sat clutching the wheel, Tomas stood up with his arms extended, moving them down and up to balance the plane. Then all three of them hummed through pursed lips to simulate the sound of an engine.

Hajnal interrupted my thoughts. "Buzsi and I remained friendly after my family moved to a different part of town. When the war was over, I wrote to her to ask about relatives, just in case someone else had lived. I also had a fiancé . . . But, thank God, I have my two sisters. We stayed together."

The same miracle, I thought. Almost no one survived alone, but they did in pairs or groups.

"Well, in this letter," Hajnal went on, "Buzsi wrote to me about your little brother. It seems that her Tomas never stopped talking about him. Here, I'll read it." She found the place in the letter and looked up at us, not sure if she should continue.

> Tomas is almost nine and in third grade. I worry about him sometimes. The war had a great influence on him; he was always very impressionable and sensitive. He tends to fantasize a lot. He lives in two worlds. Do you recall the Davidowitz family across the street? They had a boy, Sandor, the same age as Tomas. They used to be pals, before the restrictions came and things fell apart. Well, Tomas won't give him up; he still talks to him in his games. When he gets home from school, he goes to look for Sandor. Strangers live

> in their house, but Tomas won't listen to reason. "Sandor is coming home in an airplane," he insists, no matter what his father and I tell him.

Hajnal stopped reading. "There is more, but I think you have heard enough."

Iboya and I had not looked at each other during the reading, but we exchanged teary glances when Hajnal stopped. My little brother shall forever remain six, I thought, while Tomas and the others grow up. I remembered how upset Sandor had been when he turned six and was not allowed to attend school, and swallowed my tears in silence.

"Still," Hajnal spoke, "it is good that they are not forgotten."

By Monday morning, walking to the match factory with Hajnal, Magda, and Iboya, I did not feel so lonely. I was assigned to a machine that made boxes for wooden matches. As the boxes came off a conveyor belt, I had to pick out the bad ones and guide the rest into cases. It needed complete concentration and electric speed. If I idled for a second, the boxes would pile up, choking the machine. I was glad when the day ended.

The Jonkoping match factory exported matches to many countries, including America. My machine and I stood in a vast room with eleven other women, each one responsible for different stages of manufacturing. There were daily fires sparked by the phosphate. Fire extinguishers were in constant use. Smoke and phosphate odor hung in the room like a permanent curtain, exceeding the rubber and glue fumes at the raincoat factory many times over. The workers coughed, cursed, and carried on with resigned acceptance. A female supervisor, weaving between the machines, made sure that our eyes and hands were always occupied by work. She did not tolerate gossip between the women.

It was very difficult for me to keep my mind on the machine. My thoughts would take flight without any warning, and my machine would choke and sputter, grinding up and spitting boxes like a sick monster. By the time I reached for the off switch, it would usually have stopped from congestion. The mechanic and supervisor would rush over, yelling and gesticulating in anger. Luckily I could not hear their words over the noise of the running machines. During lunch in the factory cafeteria, the other workers would tease me: "So you were off dreaming again." Iboya would be embarrassed and beg me not to do it again. Her machine boxed the wooden matches. It required more skill than mine, yet she had no problems.

Iboya was afraid that I would be fired. Our combined salaries just about covered the essentials of our living expenses, with a little left over for clothes and an occasional treat for sweets or a film. The Swedish women always complained about the hardship of trying to manage on their meager salaries. They also had taxes to pay. We were exempt on account of our not being citizens. The five dollars a month we got from HIAS, a Jewish charity organization, was put in a special kitty for stationery, postage, toiletries, and an occasional bus ride to visit Suri and other friends in the camp outside Göteborg. The Swedish Red Cross still looked after our medical needs. A young woman named Margaret would come twice a month and take me to a clinic to have my feet treated for frostbite from our six-week winter march.

To get to and from the factory from our rooming house, we walked through an open market. I often lingered by the fresh fruit and vegetable stalls, and asked Iboya if we could buy a red tomato, an apple, or some grapes. She sometimes gave in, with reluctance, for these items on a factory worker's salary were considered luxuries. I was surprised, since in Hungary during the summer months fruits and vegetables were plentiful. When I asked one of the Swedish women in the factory about the high prices, she explained that since Sweden has little sun, a lot of their produce is imported.

On Saturday evenings, the handful of Jewish families in town got together and arranged dances for us. Some of their sons and daughters formed a musical group and served refreshments. Here we met the male refugees who worked at various jobs in the city. They were mostly German and Polish; there were very few male Hungarian survivors. We looked forward to these get-togethers, they gave us a chance to socialize. Soon marriages formed of various national combinations. We knew a German father with two sons who acquired a Polish and a Hungarian daughter-in-law and a Czechoslovakian wife. They all lived together in a rented house. The old man was trying to teach the three women German, while they insisted he learn Hungarian, Polish, and Czech. Iboya and I were friendly with the Hungarian daughter-in-law and visited the small house on occasion. They all liked to play cards and took their game very seriously. If a fight erupted, they argued in four languages. When the older son and his Hungarian wife had a baby, the child learned words in German, Hungarian, Polish, Czech, and Swedish.

I became friends with one of the few Jewish Swedes during the dances. Zigi was ten years my senior. He was an engineer at the boatyards. Though not one of the regulars at our socials, he would stop in from time to time. There was a mystery about him. He would appear at an unpredictable hour, stay for a while, and then disappear. He always managed to ask me to dance at least once during his stay. After a while, I found myself watching the door and felt disappointed at the end of an evening if he did not show up.

We spent Sundays doing our laundry, visiting, and writing letters. Iboya wrote most of the letters to Etu and Geza. After a long wait, they had been put on a boat with several hundred passengers bound for Palestine, but their ship had been turned away by the British and they wound up in Cyprus, where they now lived in a refugee camp. Etu sounded very unhappy. Being back in a camp atmosphere was the last thing they needed, and living conditions were harsh and primitive.

David was dealt the same fate. His letters spoke of frustration and anger at the British. He lost all the enthusiasm of his first letter. "You were smart not to be persuaded," he wrote. "I hope you get in touch with your American relatives and start a new life." I found it hard to answer his letters. I would sit and stare at the blank stationery and finally fill it with the trivia of our daily routine. What encouragement could I offer him? He knew the political struggle of the Jews better than I. They were still fighting the British and the Arabs in order to gain control of and govern Palestine. The situation looked hopeless. The fighting was continuous and the casualties high. Eventually our letters lost energy and became less and less frequent.

A few days before Rosh Hashanah, Iboya and I came home from work and found Dora waiting for us. I knew from her letters that she and Hershi were having problems and that she might come for a visit, but I was shocked by her appearance. Her body was puffy, her face depressed, and her blue eyes listless. She and I went for a walk so we could talk. "I suppose you guessed I'm pregnant."

"I wasn't sure," I said. "Why don't you get married?"

"Hershi is afraid of the responsibility. Pali is telling him that we could not manage on our own. He could never support a family on his salary."

"So what are you going to do?"

"I'm giving the baby up for adoption. There is a rabbi in Göteborg who is looking for a good family."

I was speechless, so Dora went on. "We've saved hardly any money. I have been sick from the pregnancy and lost my job." Dora took out a pack of cigarettes and started to smoke. I noticed her fingers were stained with nicotine. "Do you think that . . . I mean, would it be all right if I stayed with you and Iboya for the Holy Days? I don't want to go to the home until I have to."

"What home?"

"A home for unwed mothers. It is about a two-hour bus ride from here." Seeing my expression, Dora added, "I could not write you these things in a letter!"

I felt so sorry for my dear friend that I wanted to hug her, but we were both on the verge of tears and I knew that we would have broken down. Forcing my voice to be natural, I assured her that it would be all right for her to stay.

When we returned from our walk, I saw the older women in our building giving Dora side glances, looking at her stomach and whispering. I knocked on Magda's door to introduce Dora, knowing she would understand. Magda's sister Elza opened the door. The first thing that hit me, at eye level, was a two-inch silver cross hanging from around her neck. We ran into each other's arms.

"What are you doing here?" I cried.

"I came for Rosh Hashanah. Come in, come in and sit down. I just visited Iboya while you were out walking." After I introduced Dora, we moved over to the square table with four chairs. Magda poured us some milk.

"I can't believe how pretty you look," Elza told me. "Not a trace of your sufferings show. Nobody could guess, just as if it had never happened," she mused, fingering her cross. My eyes were drawn to her body, all filled out with muscle and flesh, like any normal person's. Elza made a sucking sound with her lips and shook her head in wonder.

Dora, sensing the direction of our thoughts, got up and said we would have to be going. I led her into our room and announced to Iboya, "Dora is going to stay with us over the holidays." Iboya did not look too pleased; I knew she was worried about what people would say. "She will share my bed," I said, ignoring her disapproval. I hardly slept that night for fear of hurting the baby.

The Jewish families got a rabbi from Stockholm, as was their custom, and were to hold services in a large rented hall. They invited us refugees to join them. On Rosh Hashanah eve, as we were getting ready to go, Dora was hesitant, not wanting all eyes focused on her stomach. "You two go and I'll stay here and write some letters. I'm not used to celebrating or praying. My mother did not observe the holidays."

Being in the makeshift synagogue felt strange; this was the first confrontation with a place of worship for Iboya and me since we left home. At the school, we had just the festivities without the worship. Mixed emotions about God and religion surfaced.

The hall had a curtain dividing the men from the women, in the Orthodox fashion. We found it strange, since the Swedish Jews looked anything but Orthodox. There was some protest from the refugees. My attention was distracted from their heated discussion when I noticed Zigi among the congregation. Our eyes met and he came over to speak to me, followed by a blond, suntanned man around the same age. Zigi introduced him as Rulle. Rulle had a nice build and wore an impeccably tailored gray suit with a white shirt that enhanced his deep tan, most unusual for a Swede. "I did not expect to see you at religious services," I said to Zigi.

"My parents brought over the traditions from their childhood in Russia and Poland. As for myself, I just come along to please my mother," Zigi explained. He gestured to a middle-aged lady in a dark suit and black hat. I was aware of her watching us and felt uncomfortable.

After the services were over, I took Iboya's hand and rushed her out of the building. I did not want to meet Zigi's mother. She looked protective.

On Yom Kippur day, as Iboya and I entered the hall, Rulle was waiting for us. "My mother would like the two of you to join us for dinner, after the services."

Iboya gave me a questioning look.

"I have a friend visiting . . ." I started to make an excuse, but Iboya cut in, "She would want you to accept."

"Then it's all settled." Rulle grinned. His face was boyish despite a mustache, his eyes a friendly blue.

As we walked to his home, Rulle in the middle and Iboya and I on either side, he told us about his recent adventures. "I have just returned from a year abroad. After my father died I got restless. I also thought of all the things he did not get a chance to do. He was only fifty-four. He had come to Sweden as a young man, married my mother, worked hard while they had nine children. I have seven sisters and a brother, all married except two sisters and myself. Anyway, my father built up a successful business in textiles but never took the time to travel. He always had an adventurous mind—not many men left their native land and their families before the turn of the century. But after he got married, his energies were concentrated on his family and his business. He was very proud of his success and even content, I guess, but after he died, I did a lot of thinking about what I wanted to do with my life. I was twenty-six and had worked in my father's factory; then I became a designer and went to work for a fashion house. I was always interested in textiles and fashion, having been born into it, but I knew there was more to life. So when I got part of my inheritance and had a little money of my own saved up, I decided to get on a cruise ship heading for Australia. I had had a sort of fascination for it ever since I was a child, and I found more than I anticipated. I fell in love with Australia, especially her modern cities. I was ready to settle down and stay there, but decided to go on with my plans to see the world."

"Where else did you go?" asked Iboya, totally captivated.

"Oh, I have seen many places—Africa, America, some of Europe . . ."

"Africa?" The question popped out involuntarily. To me, Africa meant jungles and safaris, wild animals and half-dressed natives with rings in their noses and long spears.

"Africa is very nice; I especially liked Durban. It has a nice climate, too, though it can get very hot."

"Did you see any wild animals, and what about the people . . . aren't they strange?" I asked.

Rulle laughed. "I traveled mostly in cities."

Iboya seemed annoyed by my interruptions and urged Rulle, "Tell us about New York, that is where we are hoping to go."

"We only stopped in California and Canada. San Francisco is spring all year, big parks with magnificent flowers, and the panorama of hills and valleys is breathtaking."

"Were you in Paris?" I interrupted again, thinking of all the marvelous things Lyral had told us about Paris while we were in the hospital.

"No, our ship only got to Marseilles." At this, Iboya and I stopped in our tracks. Rulle stopped, too, and looked at us questioningly.

I let Iboya explain. "Our sister Etu was there recently on her way to Palestine. Well, she wanted to go to Palestine, but she wound up in Cyprus. When were you in Marseilles?"

"July, I believe," Rulle said, trying to remember.

"I bet you were there at the same time as Etu."

"But on a different mission," I said, thinking out loud.

"No matter." Iboya checked me. "When did you get back?"

"Just a few days ago, and here we are," said Rulle, pointing to a magnificent apartment house. We walked up steep marble steps to the second floor.

Fru Slobodkin and her two daughters met us in the entrance hall. Ulla was the younger, but more imposing. She was several inches taller than Iboya and I, with a statuesque frame and brown wavy hair, only eighteen, but full-bosomed. Sonya, at twenty, was more girlish, like us, with a small frame and slight curves. Her face was oblong, with dreamy eyes; her hair straight. She resembled Fru Slobodkin. The three of them welcomed us into their spacious apartment. Oriental rugs covered the parqueted floors; oil paintings and heavily carved furniture upholstered in velvet and brocade filled the living and dining rooms. The table was set for six with gold-embossed china plates, crystal, and sterling cutlery.

As I reached for my large damask napkin and carefully covered up my dress, I thought, How bizarre—here we are, in borrowed clothes, if you could call them that. Iboya had purchased a gray flannel jumper to go with her paisley blouse, and had me fitted with a wine-colored dress, so we would have something to wear to services and not look too shabby, knowing too well that we were going to return them to the store on Monday. She had saved the sales tickets, and would turn the clothes on the wrong side and press them out neatly, put them back in the box, and explain to the saleslady that we could not afford to keep them after all. I sat there surrounded by all this wealth, scared that I might spot my dress and not be able to return it.

The dishes served were the same ones my mother used to prepare for the end of Yom Kippur, except that Mother's chicken soup had noodles whereas Fru Slobodkin's had pirogis. The kugel and vegetable casseroles were very tasty, and after fasting all day, I had to remember my manners. There was an unspoken effort around the table to keep the conversation light, and yet any comparison of the dishes or traditions to home seemed jarring. Still, I was enjoying myself.

Ulla was the most inquisitive and asked a few questions, like, "Will you be staying in Sweden long or will you be going back to Hungary?" But after a few sideways glances from Fru Slobodkin, she turned her questions to Rulle. "Finish that story about the Canary Islands—did those people speak Spanish?"

"Mostly," he said.

"Then how did you communicate with them?"

"I have some understanding of the language and I had friends from the boat who translated for me."

"I wish I were a man and could take off to all those exotic places. It just isn't fair!" Ulla looked at her mother accusingly, as if she had made up the rules, and said to Iboya and me, "At least you girls have done some traveling." Then, sorry for speaking untactfully again, she added, "I so wish I could travel."

Sonya, trying to change the subject, asked, "Where in your travels did you find the girls most beautiful?"

Rulle, without the slightest hesitation, answered, "Here in Sweden first, then Denmark and Norway."

"So you don't like exotic types?" said Ulla, disappointed, and I realized that she considered herself exotic. The travelogue conversation continued through the sampling of sponge and honey cakes. After coffee, we all helped with the dishes; then Iboya and I said our thank yous and exchanged Happy New Year wishes with our three hostesses.

Walking us home, Rulle was not so talkative; he would lapse into long silences between questions about our future plans. "If I decide to stay home for a while, I would like to get active in the Saturday music group, if I'm not too rusty. I haven't played the piano for a year. Will you be there next Saturday?" He directed this question to Iboya.

"Yes, we usually look forward to it," she answered, trying to sound offhand.

After Rulle was out of earshot I said, "Well, you have a boyfriend." Iboya gave me an angry look. "I know that you like him," I persisted as she stood looking after him.

Iboya had not formed any attachments to the opposite sex since the ghetto. She had occasional dates, but remained casual with all of them. When I commented on this, she said, "We are going to America, so what would be the use of getting involved?" Suri had finally gotten a visa to join her relatives in America, and we had given her the names of our aunts and uncles and the piece of address we remembered, Bridge-port, to take with her. Iboya was sure that Suri would be able to locate them. I admired her practical attitude, but sensed that a certain change had taken place from the moment Zigi had introduced her to Rulle. Iboya seemed stunned by his presence. This morning she had taken great care with her hair before leaving for services, spending more time in front of the mirror than I could ever remember her doing. Even Dora noticed it and gave me a wink.

Now as we entered our room, Dora and Magda glanced up from their conversation and questioned us about our late return. Elza had gone to bed early. Trying to make it amusing, I gave them a rundown of our dinner at the Slobodkins'. "Well, we met this modern-day Gulliver; he had sailed the seven seas and he fell madly in love with our fair princess, Iboya." I got another angry look. I pretended not to notice and rambled on.

Dora, perceptive as usual, decided to entertain us with a new topic. "I heard from Ida last week. She is still in Visingso, but not for long. She will be moving to Stockholm soon. Six months ago, with the help of her Swedish family, she found a position as a governess to a four-year-old girl whose mother died about a year ago. The father is a dentist, and he has fallen in love with Ida. They are getting married and moving to Stockholm. She will be a Swedish mama, just what she had hoped to be. Now, isn't that a Cinderella story?" Dora's face shone with happiness for our ex-schoolmate. "She sent me a photo of her doctor husband-to-be, and he is a true Swede."

Dora proceeded to tell Magda about Ida's ambition. "From the first time I met her in quarantine, after our arrival in Sweden, she talked about wanting to stay here and never leave. While the rest of us were concerned about getting well, finding our families, starting a new life, Ida only wanted to become a Swede. She kept her eyes and ears open to the language, the mannerisms, the customs. She would stand in front of a mirror and practice the Swedish sounds. We used to laugh at her." Dora took some deep breaths through her diaphragm, imitating Ida. As fluent as some of us were in Swedish, none of us had the breathing down properly. It was a constant mystery to us the way they spoke, with their sighs punctuating the sounds. But most of us didn't even try; we were content just to learn the words.

"Why is Ida so determined to lose her identity? What is she afraid of, or does she have a reason to hide?" Magda asked with a skeptic's curiosity.

"It's not her, really, it's her . . ." Dora was going to divulge something, but looked over at Iboya and changed her mind. Dora was intimidated by Iboya.

Magda rushed in to ease the awkward silence. "I should not have questioned Ida's motives. After all, look at us. We're not planning to return home." After Magda went back to her room, the three of us prepared for bed without any further discussion.

By the time Dora was ready to depart for the home for unwed mothers, I had gotten used to her company again and hated to see her leave. On her last morning with us, while she was out of the room, I asked Iboya, "Don't you think that Pali is a monster, trying to run Hershi's life? Just because he saved a life, it does not mean he owns it."

Iboya's voice was scolding. "It all depends on the way you look at it. Pali feels responsible for Hershi. He is older and realizes what a struggle it would be for them to raise a child when they don't even have a chance to grow up themselves. We have not observed them living with each other. Perhaps they have been fighting since this added burden. It could destroy their feelings for each other. We have no right to judge. Maybe Pali is trying to save them from making another mistake."

Iboya's speech was finished. It was my turn to stick up for Dora. "Well, you can believe that if you want to, but

I think Pali is just trying to keep Hershi for himself."

Iboya and I walked Dora to an early bus on our way to work. She looked very alone as we left her at the bus stop, in spite of her joking farewell: "Well, don't work too hard and make me feel guilty going on a holiday." That was Dora; she would never let us feel sorry for her.

Rulle became a regular at the Saturday socials. He played the piano, took breaks from the band, and danced with Iboya. After the refreshments, he walked us home. Zigi also started to show up more frequently. Sometimes he would stay till the music ended, and the four of us would leave together, stopping at a coffeehouse on the way home.

It was a new experience—double-dating with Iboya. She allowed herself to act more as my peer than as my mother. We had gone out with boys together before, in the ghetto; Iboya with Shafar, Judi with Gari, and I with Henri, but that was a different setting altogether; a different world, it now seemed.

Thinking of Henri, I wondered again whether he was alive. Did he remember his promise to me to get back together after the war?

Zigi was very unlike Henri. First of all, he was a full-grown man of twenty-five. Then he was Swedish, untouched by the scars of war. While we were in the ghetto, he was in engineering school, studying, skiing, boating, and no doubt dating many university girls. But he did not look like a Swede with his dark straight hair, olive skin, and mysterious smile that mirrored his personality.

He loved soccer and helped organize a team of the

male refugees, giving me the title of nurse and putting me in charge of the first-aid kit. I hoped none of them would break a leg, since there was very little I knew about setting one, but I was glad to have an excuse to hang around all the practices and games.

Rulle did not get involved with soccer. He was more interested in teaching Iboya to play bridge. They would also go to the cinema and he often invited us both to his house, where he would play magician. After dinner he would dim the lights in the living room and perform magic to entertain Sonya, Ulla, Iboya, and me. One of his favorite tricks was done with a man's black umbrella. He would make it stand suspended, and then command it to obey his orders. The umbrella would waver at first, but then it performed as directed. I sat in the darkened room listening to the magic words that hypnotized the umbrella, completely caught in the spell. Rulle told us that he had learned this hypnosis from a magician in Africa and that he could perform it on people as well, but he did not get any volunteers from among us. It was a long time before I found out his secret was black thread.

Iboya was mesmerized in a different way. Rulle had great influence on her. She started dressing in a sophisticated style to complement his. Most of the clothes came from his sister, Sara, who was married to a prominent doctor. Rulle and Iboya played bridge and socialized with them. All winter Rulle wore a smart gray topcoat, a gray homburg, and gray suede gloves. At his side was Iboya in a fashionable fur-trimmed black suit, a black felt picture hat, and black suede boots. With her blond hair, she cut quite an impressive figure.

Those were her dating clothes—on Monday Iboya and I went back to being factory girls. I had more and more problems with daydreaming at work and getting into trouble with my machine and the supervisor.

After one of these episodes, we came home to find an airmail letter for us from America—from New York. Both of us knew instantly that it was good news. I waited excitedly while Iboya ripped open the envelope. We both tried to read it at the same time.

February 16, 1947

Dear Iboya and Piri,

You can't imagine how happy we are to find out that two of our nieces survived the war. I just came home from a party given by a friend of mine for a niece who came from Sweden, and it turned out that Suri is a friend of yours. Suri was telling us that she wanted to put an ad in the Jewish paper for two girls from Beregszász. Knowing that my husband, your Uncle Sam, had a sister living in Beregszász, I asked for the names. Well, I could hardly believe it when she told me who you were. I ran to the telephone and called your uncle. He called his sister Regina and her husband, David, in Bridgeport. She called her brother Morris and his wife, Eva, in Los Angeles. You also have an Auntie Rose and Uncle Libe in Brooklyn, but we decided not to call them because Rose has a bad heart. We better tell her in person. I'll go see her tomorrow. Since she was the last one to emigrate and remembers you best, it will be too much of a shock for her. We have all been hoping that someone from your family was alive, but could not find out anything. Suri tells us that you are two beautiful girls, and miraculously in good health. We can hardly believe it, knowing what you have been through. The four families will get together in trying to bring you to America, then we will write and tell you what can be done. We will also help you financially till we can get you out. Write and tell us how we can be of help.

Stay well and don't worry about anything.
Your Auntie Simi

Iboya and I exploded with joy. We hugged and danced about our room. Magda came to see what all the noise was about. She called out to the others in the house, and they all shared in celebrating our good news. The upstairs women came running down the long flight of steps, crowding our room and hallway. This happened whenever one of us located a relative. But there was a certain sadness with the joy, because of the many who were still searching without success and because every passing day reduced their chances of finding a loved one.

After supper, as Iboya pulled out one of our air letters from her stationery box and sat down to write the first letter to America, I noticed a perplexed expression on her face. I guessed it had to do with Rulle. They were in love, and after all her plans and waiting, now she was confused. But none of this showed in the letter when she gave it to me to read. She conveyed only gratitude and the hope of emigrating to America.

A few days later, while I was fantasizing about becoming an American woman and trying on different costumes I had seen on Claudette Colbert and Ingrid Bergman in American films, my machine choked again. Frantically I tried to fix it before the supervisor was called. As I looked up to see if she was nearby, I noticed a middle-aged couple staring at me in sympathy. I reached for the paste bottle, trying to pretend the paste was too thick and that was what had caused the clogging.

I was stirring away vigorously, turning my back on the sympathetic onlookers, when the man spoke in a fatherly tone of voice: "It is not the glue. Try to turn the wheel in reverse."

Since I had seen the mechanics do it for previous congestions, I shut off the switch and tried to move the wheel manually. I couldn't master it.

"I would help, but it is against the rules for visitors to touch the machines."

"Thanks anyway," I said, still struggling, when the supervisor arrived at the scene.

This time the lady spoke up: "It is almost lunchtime; would it be all right to invite the young lady to join us?"

"The workers eat at our cafeteria," came the supervisor's abrupt reply.

"That is just what we are about to do. You see, we are with a tour and we have our lunch tickets." The lady held up two yellow meal tickets. Just then the bell rang and all speech was drowned out by the rush of the workers.

The prematurely gray-haired lady took my sticky hand and guided me through the crowd. I realized as we reached our table that I had forgotten to remove my rubber apron. Further embarrassed, I excused myself to go to the washroom. The lady followed me. I took off my apron and washed the glue from my fingers.

She reached out and smoothed my hair. "How old are you?" she asked.

"Seventeen," I lied, not knowing why. My birthday was not till June.

"You are too young to work in a factory," she commented, touching my hair again. I wished I had a comb. In the murky glass over the sink, my hair looked frizzy and unkempt.

When we got back to the table, there were three trays of food waiting. I looked around for Iboya. We spotted each other and she came to join us. "This is my sister Iboya," I said as she put down her tray.

The man got up and reached for her hand. "We should introduce ourselves. I'm Allan Rantzow and this is my wife, Anna."

It was my turn. "I'm Piri."

They both tried to repeat my name, pronouncing it with the Swedish intonation. I giggled nervously and soon we were all laughing, glad to break the tension. We started our lunch, the usual tasteless concoction. They pretended to enjoy it to please me, as if I had cooked it.

Herr Rantzow put down his fork first, cleared his throat to make sure he had our attention, and spoke. "I work for the railroad and we travel free. We visit different parts of the country whenever we get the time. My wife, Anna, likes to see the way things are made, so we stop at different factories during our travels. We were here a few months ago." He paused to organize his thoughts.

Fru Rantzow cut in: "You were having trouble with your machine then, too, and probably did not notice us. I have been thinking of you since—so young to be standing by that big machine. I kept wondering if you would like to come and live with us. I did not know that you had a sister."

I was speechless, so she went on: "We have four sons, three married and one in military service. We have a nice house in the country with plenty of room."

"You would be good company for my wife; she gets lonesome by herself," Herr Rantzow explained. Iboya's cat's eyes, as Mother used to call them, lit up.

"Where do you live?" she asked.

"In Astorp; it is a small hamlet in Skane. Have you ever heard of it?" Herr Rantzow asked.

"No, how far is it from here?"

"Not far by train, and I could get you railroad tickets for visits."

Iboya looked at me questioningly, her eyes retaining the enthusiasm. I felt like a calf at market. "What about America?" I asked her.

Iboya explained to them about our newfound relatives, then turned to me and said, "All that will take a long time. Remember how long the quota list is. It took Suri almost two years."

Fru Rantzow's gentle hand reached over and touched mine. "You could come and try it for a while and see if you like us." I was glad when the bell rang to signal the end of our lunch break. I felt really uncomfortable. They said they would meet us outside at 5:00 P.M. and we could have dinner.

"That would solve our problem," said Iboya, as she walked me back to my now-fixed machine.

"Just like that, you would let me go and live with strangers, and so far away?"

"Fru Rantzow looks like an angel, and Herr Rantzow reminds me of Father with his shy manner. Besides, we have not met a Swede yet who was not kind to us. Do as they suggested. Try it for a while, and if you don't like it, you would at least have had a vacation from work. They live in a small hamlet. It sounds nice and peaceful, and you would probably have a good wholesome diet. Fresh fruits and vegetables, and things we can't afford. I worry about your health a lot. I heard from some of the girls on the waiting list for America that if you're not in perfect physical shape, you can't get a visa. They even check your teeth for cavities."

"Are you telling me that I might not pass?" I asked.

"No, but I think the Rantzows are a godsend. They came at just the right time."

Iboya had a date with Rulle that evening, so I had dinner with the Rantzows alone—my first experience with a real restaurant, except for once as a child, when my mother's brother died and she rushed off to catch a train to Budapest, leaving Father to take us out to dinner. Now I felt very ill at ease and thought everyone was looking at me. I always stood out wherever I went because of my coloring. With the whole population so fair, my dark hair and eyes appeared black.

I also did not know how to order. My speech was fairly good, but reading was another matter. I was not familiar with Swedish dishes and was utterly confused. The only purpose the large menu served was to hide my distressed face behind it. Herr Rantzow took over and ordered for all three of us.

During the meal, they did their best to convince me to come as soon as possible. I took their address and said I would write.

Several more letters came from America; all of them promised to send us affidavits guaranteeing to support us so we would not have to cut into the American job market. They sent money and a large parcel of clothing, judging the sizes from our photographs. Iboya and I were pretty much the same size, and since they did not specify, we each picked what suited us best. Among the large assortment we found a print dress almost identical to the one Dora was wearing when we first met her in Lübeck. As I held it up Iboya said, "That's Dora." Knowing hers had worn out beyond repair, we wanted to make her a present of this one and a few other items. We could afford to be generous now that both Iboya and I were well dressed.

We decided to pay Dora a visit and give her the clothes. She would not come to Jonkoping because she felt too self-conscious, being eight months' pregnant now, and she did not want us to come to the home either, so we met at her bus station. It was a gray drizzly day and she was really glad to see us. She couldn't get over our new clothes and was thrilled with the ones we brought her. We sat on a wooden bench and she told us that the arrangements had been made for a childless family to take her baby. "They are very well off, the rabbi tells me, and can't wait to have the baby. They can afford to give him a good education and all the comforts, so in a way I'm lucky. They know all about me, but this is all that I know about them."

She folded her arms high over her stomach. "At times I wish it was all over, but then again, I wish I could carry him forever."

Dora's coat did not meet in the middle. She tried to cover her protruding stomach by pulling it closed, but a six-inch space remained exposed. On a sudden impulse, she took my hand and placed it inside her coat. "You want to feel him? He is moving right now." Sure enough, there was a rumbling motion under my touch. The sensation transferred into my own stomach. Dora sat very still, looking up at me, waiting for my comment.

I was embarrassed by the experience. "Why do you always refer to the baby as him?" I asked.

"The doctor said he has a boy's heartbeat."

The doctor had guessed right; Dora came to visit us for Passover with a darling baby boy. He looked just like Hershi, with pinkish-red hair, milk-white skin, and blue eyes. Dora sat nursing him while she explained, "The home allows us to keep them for six weeks if we are undecided, and I just can't bring myself to sign those papers . . ." I certainly could understand how she felt. Jani, as she had named him, felt soft as velvet and smelled like spring. He made me recall my little sister Joli as a baby. I rubbed his sausage-like arm up and down my face, then reluctantly gave him to Iboya.

"Does Pali still write to you?" Dora asked.

I took out my latest letter and handed it to her.

"He doesn't give up," Dora said, as she finished reading it. "It is strange how persistent they are till they have you, and then . . ." Her voice trailed off in sadness.

"Doesn't Hershi write to you?"

"Not the way he did before. It is a different relationship, more of an obligation. I caused him problems. His letters are not affectionate. Mostly he asks how I'm managing; he sends me some money from time to time."

"He has not seen the baby?" I asked.

"No, he said there is no point to it. I think he is afraid that if he saw him, he could not give him up. I really tried to talk him into coming or letting me come to Stockholm, but he wrote back that he had made up his mind not to see the baby."

Before Dora left, Iboya and I lent her some money to telephone Hershi, giving him a last chance to change his mind. It did not work. He only made her cry.

When Dora hung up, she took a deep breath and said, "Well, I guess it's final. I just have to do it. I can't take care of him by myself." Anger at Hershi made her determined. Suddenly her face looked many years older and not so pretty. There was nothing else we could do for her. We shared some more of our American clothes with her. "I'll wear them to Stockholm," she said as she folded them up in her bag with the baby's things.

"You still love him?" I asked as I walked her to the bus.

"I wish I didn't," she answered, with the same bitter expression.

I was depressed for days after Dora left, and I never wrote to Pali again. He sent me a few registered letters, but I refused to accept them.

Fru Rantzow wrote and urged me to come. "The countryside is beautiful at this time of year; we know that you would be happy here. We miss you." She signed it "with love." Iboya started to sort our clothes as soon as she finished reading the letter, giving me more than my share.

"I appreciate your being so generous, but I can't help thinking that you can't wait to get rid of me," I told her. "I'm still not sure that I want to go. It seems that as soon as I get used to a place, I have to start all over again. Suppose I don't fit in with these people. How do I tell them, 'I don't feel comfortable here'? It will sound very ungracious."

"Listen, Piri, I know you tell everyone that you survived only because of my looking after you. Well, nobody could deny that each of us survived by taking strength from the other. However, I also need to tell you that, in your case, personality had a lot to do with it. You have a way of getting along with people. You capture their sympathy and win them over. Mother recognized this trait in you." Iboya looked up at my surprised face. "She couldn't tell you this because she did not want you to be conscious of it. It had to be natural and spontaneous. What I'm trying to say is, you will not have any problems fitting in with the Rantzow family."

The next day, as the two of us walked to the railroad station, Iboya told me, "Last night when Rulle's mother found out that you were going off to Astorp, she invited me to come and share the large bedroom with Ulla and Sonya. So now we are both going to live with families." Iboya set my suitcase down near the first window seat, in the third car from the locomotive. Mother used to choose that seat for us when we traveled on our own to Komjaty to visit Babi. She called it the safest. "In case of trouble, you would not be too near the engine, and it is the easiest seat to get out of."

Iboya did not hug me. I felt abandoned, though I understood that she did not want us to get emotional in front of the other passengers. We had learned that the Swedes are very reserved. Iboya's farewell words were "You must be frank with me in your letters and tell me how you like it there."

The Rantzows' house was on a quiet street with neighbors close by. It had three bedrooms upstairs, a living room, dining room, and kitchen on the main floor, with a front and rear entrance, and the brand-new indoor bathroom had a toilet and a sink. They were very proud of that. Not everybody in Astorp had indoor plumbing. It felt good living in a house again.

I had arrived in Astorp toward the middle of May, and a week later there was a party in my honor. All the family and their minister were invited. Anders, the oldest, was a big man, towering over his father. He had a good nature and in looks took after his mother. His wife, Britta, was a tall, striking woman, quiet and very reliable. Fru Rantzow called her "the stable one." They had a twelve-year-old son.

Knut, the second son, seemed most like Herr Rantzow, both in appearance and personality. The favorite uncle, he was always making jokes and knew how to make each of the children feel special. He and his wife, Gunborg, lived nearby in a recently built house with two indoor bathrooms, one of which had a bathtub and shower. "You come and take your bath at our house whenever you feel like it," he invited me. Gunborg was a practical, hardworking woman, determined to keep her office job till the house was built and furnished before starting a family. "The way Knut likes children, I'm not so sure that she has made the right decision," I had heard Fru Rantzow say.

Arne, the Rantzows' third son, did not resemble any of the other members of the family. He had white-blond hair and was delicate in build compared to the rugged Rantzow males. His wife, Gun, seemed nervous trying to keep their two young children under control.

The youngest son, Nore, was the darling of the family; all of them doted on him. He looked dashing in his army uniform—square shoulders, small waist, long legs. In the middle of the evening, though, he changed into casual slacks and a sport shirt, and rolled on the living-room rug, roughhousing with his niece and two nephews. His "fiancée," as Greta had introduced herself to me the first day I arrived, when she came to have a look at me, was somewhat matronly—too mature for a boy so playful. She was the manager of her parents' fabric store in the village of Astorp, and asked me to stop in whenever I was in the neighborhood. She also offered to teach me to ride a bike, after she had gotten over the shock of Fru Rantzow's words: "Piri can't ride a bicycle." In Sweden, the idea of a grown person not being able to ride was unheard of.

Fru Rantzow had showed her annoyance at Greta's coming over uninvited on my arrival. "She couldn't wait, her jealousy got the best of her," she commented to Herr Rantzow as Greta left. Herr Rantzow answered his wife with a scolding look. Greta was not her choice, I guessed.

Now Nore tried to get me to join him on the floor to play with the children. Too many eyes were watching, and I was most conscious of Greta's. Besides, I was not yet that comfortable in my new environment. They all were a family and I was an outsider. I felt like the little girl who fell off the gypsy wagon.

Back home in Hungary, my brother-in-law Lajos used to tease me that I was really adopted because I had the darkest and only curly hair in the family. "A big gypsy caravan went through Beregszász one night and left you behind. In the morning Mother found you and figured, 'Well, I have four daughters already, so one more won't make much difference.' "

I declined Nore's invitation to play with the children and busied myself helping Fru Rantzow in the kitchen. The minister invited me to sit with him at dinner, and asked me if I could speak Hebrew.

"I was taught to read it when I was a child," I said, "but I'm afraid the lessons were in vain. I don't think I remember any of it. I was not interested and only half concentrated to please my mother."

He told me that he had learned it in the seminary and kept up with it. "I like to read the Old Testament in its original form. None of the translations is accurate." Now I felt embarrassed. "Of course, if you don't understand the meaning of the words, you can't feel enthusiastic," the minister offered sympathetically. "There is a Jewish doctor in the village and sometimes we get together and practice."

Was he the token Jew in Astorp till I came, I wondered. After the party I made an entry in a diary given to me by Adele, a co-worker at the match factory, and signed it G.G., for Gypsy Girl. It soothed me.

Nore went back to the army after that weekend, and I became Fru Rantzow's constant companion. She took me visiting friends, shopping, and attempted to teach me quilting, her passionate hobby. One of the bedrooms was taken up with her huge frame. It could accommodate a double-size quilt. She gave quilts as gifts for all occasions.

I'm certain of her disappointment at my lack of interest, even though she was very careful about not showing it. I talked about getting a job. I felt useless and my mind started working overtime, which always scared me. I was tossing at night, unable to sleep.

I did like helping in the kitchen. Fru Rantzow was an excellent cook and baker, and I soon learned her skills and introduced her to what I knew of my mother's. There were days when she was laid up with kidney-stone attacks and I could take over the cooking without much trouble. I also enjoyed cleaning the house. I found in washing and dusting a certain tranquillity. In that way, I reminded myself of my older sister Rozsi. She would open the small windows to air Babi's house on the farm while she went about her chores and I could hear her singing while I played with my friend Molcha in the garden. The Rantzows appreciated my helping out and bought me gifts of pretty clothes.

One day Herr Rantzow, who treated me as a ten-year-old at times and sang Swedish songs to me while I sat on his lap, noticed with shock that I was not a little girl and asked Fru Rantzow to get me a brassiere. From the good food and easy life, I started to fill out at last. When Fru Rantzow took me to be fitted, she commented, "A waste of money; they don't need any support." But I was very pleased to have developed, knowing that the Germans had mixed some drugs into our tea concoction to stop us from menstruating because of the lack of facilities to take care of ourselves. The brassiere might not have been needed for support, but it reassured me that all was well with my body.

A petite blond girl named Lisa lived across the street. I often watched as she got picked up by a car with other young people in it. They sounded jolly and full of energy as they crowded into the small black car and zoomed off.

Lisa had a brother, Hasse, who, I heard from Fru Rantzow, was dating a girl from one of the wealthiest families in Astorp. "The girl's family isn't thrilled about it," she told me, "even though Fru Anderson thinks that they are pretty special themselves." I had spoken briefly to Fru Anderson on occasion as we passed on the road, and Fru Rantzow was right. She was definitely of the opinion that she was too good for Egnahemes Street. When the neighbors got together for a coffee klatch, or just stood about chatting on a sunny day, she would always find an excuse not to join them. I wondered why they even bothered asking her to come and share their fancy sweets and good coffee.

I often joined the neighbors to please Fru Rantzow and because I could eat my fill of a dozen varieties of scrumptious cookies. They took such pride in preparing them, especially because their ingredients were still a novelty. On account of the war, even the Swedes did not have all the coffee, butter, sugar, and fillings they needed for their baking. Now that these things were available again, the women were re-experimenting with their old recipes.

One day while I was returning from an errand with Alfred Parson, our spry seventy-five-year-old caretaker, the small black car pulled up across the road. A tall young man came over to me as I hopped off the luggage rack of the bicycle and asked if I would care to come along for a ride. I was very tempted, but unsure.

"Go on with you," urged Alfred Parson. "I'll tell Fru Rantzow that you have gone in the automobile." He said it as if it were a spaceship. Cars were rare in Astorp because of the war and because it was a small village. Very few people had ever driven one. I myself had been in a car only the few times that I had been transported officially by the Swedish Red Cross, so I could not resist.

The tall young man turned out to be the owner of the car and a partner in the photo studio in Astorp; his name was Erik. He had brown hair almost as dark as mine. To explain it, he told me his father was Danish. I knew that Lisa was a photographer, too; Erik was one of her bosses. Her brother Hasse was also in the car and we dropped him off at his girlfriend's house, the biggest private house I had seen in Sweden thus far. It was in an area I had not been to before, with other large houses. There was another young man in the back with Lisa and Hasse who was also connected with the studio. He seemed to be Lisa's boyfriend. After we dropped off Hasse, a more relaxed conversation developed among the four of us who remained. Mostly they asked me questions about myself. It seemed that I had been the topic of discussion in Astorp for the last month.

Don't you have any family left? How long were you in those camps? How old were you? It must have been awful . . . Every question was punctuated with their typically Swedish sigh, *oh-ha*. Lisa's doll-like face had a heightened color as she listened to me. She hung on to every word I spoke. I kept the answers simple, without much detail, not wanting to put a damper on my first ride through the countryside. And I took so much pleasure from being part of this social group that I didn't want to separate us too much by what I was saying.

After that ride, I was often included during the summer. There seemed to be about a dozen couples in the clique that took rides in "Charlie," as they had named the car (because it was American). Then Erik asked me to be his date at a party. This party was going to be given in Hasse's girlfriend's house, toward the end of the summer. Her name was Gullan. I had met her a few times, but we hardly spoke. She was the only one who treated me as an inferior, so I stayed away from her.

On the first occasion when Erik took me for a drive alone, he put his arm around me as we rode. But he treated me gingerly. I guessed that it was on account of my war experiences. Whatever it was, I was not encouraging him to go any further. I was very unsure of where I stood with his group, and I had not sorted out my feelings romantically for quite a while. My correspondence with David had stopped. I had written to him from Astorp just so he would have my address, but he did not answer. By now he was living on a kibbutz and knew that we were waiting to emigrate to America. We did not fit into each other's future. It had hurt for a while, but I understood and had gotten used to it. Saying goodbye to people I loved had become second nature to me.

Zigi wrote perhaps once a month. Then, out of the blue, he showed up at the Rantzows', just the way he would show up at one of the dances in Jonkoping. I was in the cellar where we stored our food so it wouldn't spoil. I was about to bring up some casseroles for our smorgasbord supper when I heard a motorcycle. I ran up on the double, empty-handed. It was crazy to suspect that it might be Zigi, but he had written in one of his letters that he had bought this great machine in Huskvarna and what fun he had riding it back to Jonkoping. Besides, I don't think I had seen or heard a motorcycle in all the time I had lived in Astorp. The motor was still sputtering when I reached the yard.

Alfred Parson was standing near the rabbit hutch with a basket of feed. His faded blue eyes could not have been more excited or bewildered if a man from Mars had landed. Fru Rantzow was on the back porch, wiping her hands on her apron. I ran past her and watched the rider lift off helmet and goggles. Sure enough, it was Zigi. When he opened his arms, I flew into them, forgetting the audience. It felt good to be squeezed in his sweaty embrace. After a few seconds, I pushed him away and introduced him to my Swedish mama, as I had gradually come to call her, by request. Alfred Parson still had not moved, so I dragged Zigi over to the rabbit hutch and made the introduction. Zigi tried to make some conversation about the rabbits, but Alfred Parson, as he regained his mobility, walked past him to touch the machine. He slid the helmet off the handlebar and tried it on. It covered half his face, and we all started to laugh. Fru Rantzow lost no time in being hospitable and asked Zigi to wash up and join us for supper. To me she said, "Piri, you better go and bring up the food from the cellar so we can heat it up. Your young man must be hungry from riding that heavy thing." As Mama slowly said the words "your young man," she gave me a strange look.

Zigi offered to help me bring up the casseroles. Once we were down in the dim light of the cellar, he embraced me again and we joined in a long, lingering kiss. This was a new development in our relationship. It felt good, so I decided not to question it.

I felt happier that evening than I had since I came to Astorp. At first Zigi talked about continuing on his way to some shipyard after supper, but the Rantzows talked him into spending the night. "It is threatening to rain," Papa said at supper, "and that machine would attract lightning."

Zigi and I went for a long walk after supper. He never took his arm from my shoulder. We stopped several times in the shadows and repeated the passionate kiss from the cellar. Now Zigi confessed that he had made the trip just to see me. He was not on his way to any shipyard. It started to drizzle, so we walked back to the house.

The Rantzows had gone upstairs to bed and had left

some bedding for Zigi on the sofa. We did not make up the bed but brewed some coffee and brought it into the living room. I had so many questions about Iboya and Rulle, the men on the soccer team, the people we knew from the socials—and Zigi was telling me about his building a ship. We sat on the couch sipping coffee, and talking and kissing, as we listened to the rain, which took on a serious, steady sound of splatter after midnight. I don't know what time we fell asleep, but my Swedish papa found us sleeping, fully clad, in each other's arms as he was leaving for work. He slammed the door behind him just enough to wake us before Mama came down and found us.

The next evening, while Papa and I were alone, he asked, "Do you love this man, Piri?" not wanting to pry, but wanting to play papa and offer support if I needed it. I hugged him as hard as I had hugged Zigi at parting after breakfast. "No, Papa, I can't love him. He is here today and gone tomorrow. You can't depend on him. I would only get hurt if I did."

"What kind of man is he?" Papa asked.

"His next project is to build a boat with several other engineers. They want to travel to France, to the upcoming Olympics."

"That is a big, ambitious project," Papa mused.

"Yes, he tried to tell me all about it while we sat and drank coffee last night. That is probably when I fell asleep. I don't understand much about ships."

Papa did not give up. "You don't have to understand about men building ships. What I'm talking about is your mood last night. We have never seen you so happy. You were like a butterfly."

I was surprised to hear this. I was not aware of the change being so noticeable to others. "I'm sorry if my mood is not always light; I *am* happy here."

"No, Piri, your mama and I were sorry to think that perhaps you would be happier with your own kind. You seemed to fit together more, I mean . . ."

"Papa, if you mean because we are both Jewish, that does not endear him to me more than you. That we both have dark hair—so does Erik."

"Then you love him." Papa threw up his arms, confused and helpless.

Seeing him so upset made me angry at Zigi. What had this man brought into my life yesterday that I needed so much? He was familiar, at least more than the people in Astorp. And there was a cultural bond. I could let my emotion show without being misunderstood. Papa was pacing the living room, waiting for an answer. I could not reveal my thoughts for fear of hurting him, so I exclaimed, "Excitement! He brought excitement, showing up out of nowhere." When I heard the words spoken, I realized that there was a lot of truth in that, too. I burst out laughing at myself, glad that I had not told a lie.

"Astorp is not too exciting," said Mama, joining us from the kitchen.

"Yes, it is, I was just going to tell you; Erik asked me to be his date at a party given by Gullan, Hasse's girlfriend." Mama's blue eyes glittered as she sat down on the sofa. "I think it's her birthday."

"I wonder if she knows that Erik is planning to take you to her house. You know, a Rantzow would never be invited to that house. We just are not in the same class." Papa left the living room, not wanting any part of our conversation. He probably considered it women's talk. Mama jumped up from the sofa with a sudden burst of energy. "You know that red dress from America that you have been saving all this while? Well, I think you have a chance to wear it."

I followed her to my room and tried on the red dress.

Mama zipped me up and made me turn around. She stood still for a moment, looking at me. Then she walked a few steps, and her image joined mine in the oval stand-up looking glass. Our coloring clashed, but no one reading the expression on our faces would have questioned that we were mother and daughter. She raised a hand and touched my hair, and I turned to face her. "Mama, do you think I should go?"

"You must, you will be the prettiest girl there. And pay attention to everything; then come home and wake me, so you can tell me all about it while it is still fresh in your mind." I hugged her, perhaps a little too tight, in anticipation of my first real party.

10

I took a deep breath as Erik knocked on the heavy oak door. He gave me a reassuring look as we stood waiting to be let into the party. Gullan, wearing a large smile and a red dress, swung the door open. The smile faded as soon as she saw me. For a moment I thought she was going to close the door again, but she left it open and, turning her back on us, walked off toward the crowded living room, joining a cluster of her girlfriends in elegant party dresses, with punch cups in their hands. At Gullan's approach, they turned and stared at us. Then, in slow motion, they regrouped and resumed their intimate whispers.

Lisa, standing close by with her boyfriend and Hasse, spotted us, and the three of them came over. A few other familiars waved or nodded their heads. Erik put his arm protectively around my shoulders as we followed Lisa to the punch bowl on the large table in the center of the room. All other furniture was absent except for some chairs at the short far wall and a platform in the middle of the long wall. Beside the cut-glass bowl containing an aromatic spiked fruit punch, there were party delicacies arranged on silver trays. Hasse, playing host, urged me to try some. "Thank you, they look delicious; I'll sample them later," I said, accepting a cup of punch. The five of us walked toward the chairs and sat down.

While the four of them talked shop, I looked around at the faces of the guests, mostly strangers. Then the band arrived, and to my surprise, it was Kruger's American Band, which I had heard before. The musicians were not American, but they played American music. As the singer and bass player, Kaliu, entered carrying his bass fiddle, I tried to catch his eye, but he moved with the other musicians toward the platform and did not see me. Not till I was dancing with Erik did he acknowledge my presence with a gallant bow.

"How do you know him?" Erik asked, noticing my warm smile and wave. I answered with care. "He is a friend of Nore." It was a white lie. I did meet him when I went to a dance hall with Nore and Greta, but they were not friends. Kaliu had come over to our table during their break and introduced himself. I had been staring at him while he was singing popular American songs, but when he showed up at our table, I was terribly flustered. Nore invited him to have a drink with us. Kaliu told us he was from Finland.

"Where did you learn to sing in English?" I managed to ask after a long silence.

"I lived in America for a time," Kaliu said, as if it was of no great consequence.

"I will be going to America, but can't speak a word of English."

"You learned Swedish, so when the time comes for your emigration, you'll learn English."

Our conversation was interrupted when the other musicians returned from the bar. Kaliu went to take his place alongside them on the bandstand. While singing the next song, "The Things We Did Last Summer," he never took his eyes off me. I was most uncomfortable, because of Greta and Nore's awareness of it, but extremely flattered. After the dancing was over, Kaliu walked me home. He called me on the telephone several times after that, till Mama finally invited him for a Sunday dinner, just to take a look at him. "I want to see why you keep turning him down," she said. I could not explain that up on the platform he seemed safe, but when he sang romantic songs on the way home just for me, I was frightened. "He is very old," I told her.

Kaliu came to Sunday dinner, bringing his English grammar books and offering to teach me the basics of English. He won the Rantzows over with his matter-of-fact attitude and continental charm, but I remained intimidated by him and never did accept a date.

Recalling it all as I danced with Erik, I felt very angry with myself. Why did I act so brave from a distance, when I was such a coward? I caught Kaliu's eyes on me as he began to sing "The Things We Did Last Summer" and wished I could run from the room. During the break, Kaliu came over to where I stood with Erik, Lisa, and her friend, and just as nonchalantly as the first time, he introduced himself around. He asked how the Rantzows were. I hoped he would not say anything to give me away, but he just made light conversation about the lovely party and how he preferred to play for a private group.

I relaxed and did not notice Gullan approaching us till she addressed Kaliu. She had changed her red silk dress for a blue taffeta, and with her hair brushed in an upsweep, she did not look like her former self. She looked more sophisticated and very beautiful. The dress complimented her deep blue eyes. Her soft shoulders looked like pink porcelain. I could not help but admire her composure as she spoke to Kaliu. "When they bring out my cake, I want you to sing 'Happy Birthday' while I blow out the candles and cut the first slice. After that, you'll play the song we discussed in a slow tempo while my fiancé and I start the dance. As the others join us on the floor, you can pick up the beat. You remember the song?"

"Yes, Froken Gullan, just leave it to me; I have rehearsed it with the band; we are all set." Gullan was going to say something else, but looked over at the four of us, hesitated, and turned on her high heels.

Kaliu's gaze followed her erect back; he shook his head and said, "A determined lady." Erik chuckled in agreement and said, "I would not want to tamper with her." The band was returning. Kaliu put down his punch cup. "I'll have to pick up those English grammar books one of these days," he said to me in parting. Erik gave me a sharp look.

When the huge cake, with twenty lit candles, was carried into the room by a servant, the band picked up their instruments and Kaliu sang "Happy Birthday" to Gullan. Suddenly my mind skipped, and, instead of Gullan, I saw my sister Rozsi at the same age, standing in the Komjaty station waving goodbye to me, after we had spent our last summer together. She looked small and desolate on the platform, with the flat fields and the tall pine forest in the background as far as I could see. As I rode the train I thought of her having to make the crossing back to Babi's house by herself through the dark forest. I had bad premonitions that day.

The cake was placed on the table. The twenty tiny candles flickered their separate yellow lights. I tried to read the inscription on the cake, but I saw the flames of the candles merge and flare, rising over the pink and blue icing, charring it black, till there was only flame and ash. I felt faint and leaned on Erik for support.

"Are you all right?" he asked. "You look pale."

I did not answer, but let Erik guide me through the guests. A cool September breeze stirred the trees as we reached his car.

"Would you like to walk a while first?" Erik offered.

"No, I'd rather leave." He did not drive me home but parked near a wooded country site. He came around and helped me out. We found a large rock and sat down.

Putting his arm around me, he asked, "Are you feeling better, Piri?"

"Yes, I'm much better, thank you." Actually, I felt embarrassed, hoping no one had noticed my strange behavior. "I'm sorry to have made you leave the party."

"I was ready to leave as soon as we got there, but that would have been pleasing Gullan, and I thought that you might enjoy the dancing. Maybe we danced too much, or perhaps you're not used to so many people in one room?"

"No, it had nothing to do with dancing."

"You want to talk about it?"

I felt that I owed Erik an explanation. "I had a sister . . . her name was Rozsi. She would have been twenty four Septembers ago, but she was taken away that May." It was hard to talk about her, so I stopped. Erik did not press me, but I knew he was waiting for me to go on. "I had five sisters and a brother. They all perished in Auschwitz, as far as we know, except for Iboya, whom you'll probably meet at Christmastime, and Etu, who lives in Palestine."

"Did you all go to Auschwitz together?"

"No."

"How did you and your two other sisters get out?"

I told him about it briefly and when I was finished Erik took off his jacket and put it around my shoulders. I guess I was shivering. Then we walked to the car. We did not talk much on the way home, but he was very tender and said how fortunate he was to be living in Sweden, a country without war.

Mama was sitting in the living room when I got in. I saw white blisters under her eyes and was afraid that she was coming down with one of her kidney-stone attacks. "How was the party?" she asked.

"Are you sick?" I said instead of answering her.

"No, I was just waiting up. Papa did not like you going there; he was concerned that you might be made to feel out of place."

For a simple man he was very sensitive, I thought. "I saw Kaliu; his band was playing."

"That must have cost a lot of money," Mama said, "but they can afford it."

"He asked about you and Papa."

"I bet he was jealous of Erik."

"I don't know; he said he would like to come by and pick up his books." I was sure Mama was going to get sick.

"It is too bad you don't care for him," she teased me. "He certainly likes you. But tell me about the party."

"Well, Papa was right, I did not fit in and Gullan wasn't thrilled to have me. The red dress was a mistake. She wore a red dress and changed into a blue one after a while."

Mama got up from the sofa, furious. "What a spoiled brat; she could not stand the competition."

"I don't know why—she is beautiful, and has everything."

"Did you meet her parents?"

"No, they weren't there. Lisa said she wanted to run her own party."

Mama got angrier still. "Not to have your own folks

at your birthday party. What kind of family are they? It is just as well you did not meet them." Mama sighed. "Papa was angry with me for letting you go. But I thought, Why shouldn't you have a chance to go, you are as good as they are."

"Mama, I'm different. They played kissing games and acted . . . well, childlike. I know they are older than I, but the biggest problem in their lives is school and the most important thing is dating. I felt like a misfit."

"So you did not have a good time," Mama said, looking disappointed.

"I liked the music and dancing."

"What about Erik?"

"He is nice, and very understanding, but I would not be surprised if I do not hear from him anymore. I'm not fun."

"Let's go to bed, *kära Piri.*" Mama reached out and stroked my hair and I felt better. We walked upstairs with our arms around each other.

Erik called the next morning, and the next. We continued going for rides in his car. It was a beautiful, mild autumn, and the countryside was a color field of yellows, oranges, and greens. It stayed light for several hours after he finished work. We found ourselves going back to the same spot where we had parked after the party. In the daylight we could see quite a distance from the hill. Some days I would accompany Erik on an assignment, but wherever we were, we would talk. After the time I told him about Rozsi, I would let Erik lead me into conversation about the past.

One afternoon he did all the talking. "You see, I'm different, too, not only because my father is Danish, but because I spent three years in a sanatorium. I had tuberculosis. That is where I took up photography. I also read a lot about what happened in Germany because I had met a girl at the sanatorium who had experiences similar to yours, but she could not talk about it. She was four years older than you, and she was a supervisor. I think she felt guilty for having helped the Germans carry out their work details. There might have been more to her story. I could never touch her, nor could any of the male staff at the sanatorium. She would shake and break out in a cold sweat." Erik became silent.

"What happened to her?"

"She was still there when I left. We corresponded for a while. Then she wrote that she had located a brother in Palestine and she was joining him."

"Did you like her?"

"Yes, in a way, but she was difficult to get close to."

After listening to Erik confide in me, I felt we had a lot more in common.

In October Mama finally gave in to me and approached an engineer friend about getting me a job. Herr Gustafson hired me to keep the inventory books up to date. I was happy to keep my own schedule and not feel so dependent, and going to work in a clean office was a big improvement from being a factory worker. The problem was, I had to use an adding machine. I had never seen one before, and felt threatened, as with all machines. I asked Herr Gustafson to explain how it functioned, but every time he tried, we were interrupted by a telephone or a clerk. One afternoon, I decided not to trouble busy Herr Gustafson but to teach myself by reading the manual. Not understanding it, I resorted to trial and error. I was not succeeding and became very frustrated. My whole body turned clammy, but I would not ask anyone for assistance. Because of the constant noise of the machine, I was unaware of the office emptying, till a persistent telephone kept ringing. Why doesn't anyone answer, I wondered, getting up to stop it.

Mama's anxious voice was on the wire. "Piri, is that you? Why are you still there at this hour?" I realized with a start that I was alone in the vast room, deserted by my co-workers.

"What time is it?"

"Seven forty-five. We are frantic with worry. First I thought that Erik had picked you up, but he just called."

The silence was humming around me; the windows were blacked out by the darkness outside. All the other machines were under gray covers. "Mama, I think they all left; I'm alone in this big room." Panic enveloped me.

"Go see if the doors are open; if not, bang on them and maybe the watchman will hear you. I'll hold on." I banged till my fist was sore; no one came to my rescue. Mama promised to call Erik. "Maybe if he drives up and honks by the gate, he will attract the watchman and get him to let you out."

Was I humiliated when Erik picked me up! I could not meet his eyes for several days, and never went back to work. I had been aware of them whispering about me as it was. Now I was convinced that they would interpret my being confused with my tragic past. "I understand," Herr Gustafson said when Mama called to explain that I would not be back.

As the trees lost their leaves and the weather turned damp, Erik and I confined ourselves in the evenings to the indoors, taking turns between his house and mine. His mother, Fru Olson, was a sweet-tempered, chubby lady who fretted over Erik's health. She knitted him wool vests to wear under his blazer and warned, "Don't catch a chill." His father, like Erik, was tall and sturdy in build and did not go in for making small talk. During our friendship, the Olsons and the Rantzows started to see each other socially. Both women enjoyed cooking and having people around them. Also, while the weather still held, the six of us would take long rides in Herr Olson's big car and stop at different restaurants.

On a Sunday afternoon we stopped at a place that raised their own chickens in the yard. We were asked to pick out two for our dinner. Herr Olson remarked that he thought that was barbaric and ordered a bowl of boiled shrimp. Having grown up watching my grandmother pick out her fowl for slaughter, I thought this was odd. The shrimps were served in their pink shells, with heads and tails intact. I had never seen a whole shrimp before and was repelled by them. When Herr Olson extended the bowl toward me, I declined with a shudder. He looked into my eyes with a steady gaze, till there was a spontaneous release of laughter between us, as if a balloon had burst. After that, we had no trouble communicating.

The next week's mail from Iboya contained a letter from Etu. Etu was all excited about the prospect of the United Nations General Assembly coming to Palestine to study the internal problems.

I tried discussing it with Papa, who always read the papers. "The last recommendation was to divide Palestine into a Jewish and an Arab state, with Jerusalem becoming international. Do you think such a plan could work, Papa?"

"Piri, not having any experience with war, I'm totally ignorant about what makes people fight."

Unlike Papa, I felt as if my whole experience was war, but I still didn't know what made people fight.

"Greed is the only motive," came Mama's practical comment from the kitchen.

Soon after our conversation I heard on the radio that the plan was a fiasco. The fighting continued all through the winter of 1947.

On occasion, Erik and I would go to a dance or the cinema with Lisa and her boyfriend. They were easy to be with, but most of the time we would be a twosome. We had begun to relax with each other. Knowing I cared for him, he no longer showed signs of jealousy if we met Kaliu at a dance. When Zigi wrote, telling me that the boat was near completion and inviting me to come see it, I declined. There was no use stirring up emotions again.

By December, Astorp had a thick blanket of snow covering the countryside. Alfred Parson stayed in the house most of the time. Except for caring for the rabbits and running an occasional errand, he was content to sit by the fire and warm himself like an old dog. Mama was cheerfully engaged in projects in preparation for Christmas and had not suffered an attack since the Sunday after Gullan's party. It also helped for her to get out and socialize. Papa and I tried to help with the preparations so she would not overexert herself.

Just in time for Christmas I received a parcel from America. I had asked for rice and a few delicacies still not available in Sweden on account of the war. Mama and I stored them in the cellar till Christmas dinner. From the grocer Mama got six oranges, one for each person in the family counting Nore and Alfred Parson. "We should have five," she told me, "but he gave me two for you. They are still as scarce as gold. You and Erik can eat the extra one this evening." Erik insisted on sharing it four ways.

Iboya forwarded another letter, this time from Dora, the first news from her since she had given the baby up for adoption. She was in Stockholm, back with Hershi. She had some important news.

> With both of us working, we finally have a place of our own. Pali is fuming and won't speak to us, but as long as we have each other, it really doesn't matter. We are planning to get married in the near future. Of course, I keep thinking about the baby. Soon he'll be walking and learning to say words. Hershi was right not to see him; it saved him the pain of loving him. Yet I'm glad I had him, at least for a little while. Sometimes when I pass mothers in the park playing with their children, I want to drop everything and run to Göteborg and search the streets for him (I think that is where he lives). Then I tell myself he is better off where he is.

I was both sad and happy for Dora—sad about the way she missed the baby, and happy that at least she had Hershi, knowing how she loved him. I answered her right away, consoling her with thoughts of having another baby with Hershi.

Nore came home a few days before Christmas. He was to stay till after New Year's. We kissed and hugged so naturally that I caught Mama and Papa looking at us in surprise. Greta was busy at the store, so Nore and I washed the dishes after supper and then played dominoes. I felt none of the uneasiness of an outsider anymore. I had become part of his family. In his absence I had also become friendly with Greta, and she no longer felt threatened by my presence.

Nore seemed to know all about Erik from Greta's letters and asked me if I was still planning to join my American relatives.

"I have no choice."

"Sure you do; you have a family here now, you no longer need them."

"I'm committed; they went to a lot of trouble, sending

us affidavits, money, and packages. They are expecting us."

"Nonsense, you don't even know those people. You know us and you know that you are welcome to stay." Mama was ironing a tablecloth, her ears perked, and Papa was pretending to read the papers. Nore went on: "What about Erik, doesn't he count? Greta tells me he really cares for you. He is a sensitive young man; he has had some . . . well, I don't know how much he has told you about himself."

"He told me about the sanatorium."

"Sure, he was even turned down by the army. I don't think he's ever had a girlfriend since. It would hurt him a lot if you just up and left him." Nore dropped his dominoes. He was watching me and waiting for an answer.

I was perplexed. "He knows I'm leaving; it is understood."

"Is that what he told you?"

"We don't talk about it."

"What do you talk about?"

"You are being harsh and too personal," Papa said, and folded up the newspaper. I was grateful to have Papa put an end to Nore's insinuations and questioning, but Nore was too wound up to be put off.

"What about you and Mother," he addressed Papa. "How will you take it? I can see how you two feel about her. Mother is a changed person since Piri has come to live with us. I would be jealous if it wasn't that, actually, I have gotten used to her myself. I guess we all needed a girl in the family." Nore went on as if I had left the room. "They don't care if she comes to America; they are inviting her out of obligation."

"They are her family." Mama came over and sat down next to me on the sofa, abandoning her tablecloth. Nore looked at us for a long moment. He threw up his arms, took his coat, and walked out.

An uncomfortable distance kept Nore and me apart for the next few days. I was the little gypsy girl again, and it was lonely. Then Iboya arrived and everyone put their best foot forward to show a congenial family unity. Mama cleverly saved the Christmas baking till last, so the three of us could cut and decorate cookies together. We dressed the tree and prepared a spicy white sauce for the lutefisk, a traditional Christmas fish course. Mama had brought home the whole dried fillets of ling weeks before. She soaked them one week in water and one week in lye, till they were soft and slippery. I was not looking forward to tasting it.

By the time the rest of the clan arrived, the table was set and the feast was ready to be served. The lutefisk sat beside jellied pigs' feet, rice porridge, and an assortment of herrings, ham, and breads arranged on the sideboard. Iboya was drawn into the household by all the preparation and was totally relaxed with Mama, Papa, and Nore. But as we were seated at the table, I noticed her shyness toward the other members of the family.

When we were alone that night, Iboya remarked, "They have adopted you; they treat you as part of the family. I had no idea how things were with you."

For some reason, I felt accused. "But I told you in my letters how much they cared for me."

"Still, this is remarkable; I just can't believe you blending in with strangers . . ."

"They're not strangers!" I tried to make her understand, but in the end I realized this part of my life was separate from hers.

On one of our walks during Iboya's visit, we got into a rare discussion about Germany. We were still too vulnerable to talk much about it.

"Can you believe us in this setting?" Iboya asked. "A Swedish countryside, and we are strolling along almost as if we belonged here. You are chatting away in Swedish as naturally as if it were your native tongue. Does it seem possible that only two and a half years ago . . ." Iboya stopped and became absorbed in her thoughts.

"Some days I wake up and I think I'm in Komjaty," I said. "It all seems so familiar and comfortable. Then, as reality hits me, I can't believe it ever happened. How could we have overcome such an experience? Are we really that strong? I would think we would be crippled beyond recovery."

"Many are—we are the lucky ones. Sometimes I can still hear them screaming from the psychiatric ward across the road from the hospital. Remember how we could hear their cries night and day?"

"No, I don't want to remember. If I have to go back there, I would rather reflect on the sound of Lyral's voice. I wonder what happened to her."

"That postcard from Italy is the last I heard from her," Iboya replied. "She was still searching for her daughter. Her mother had died a few months earlier. Poor Lyral."

"Do you still have that address?"

"Yes, I put it in my little book, though she said it was temporary and that she would write as soon as she got back to France. But I never heard from her."

"Let's send a Christmas card to that address in Italy," I said. "What can we lose?" When we got back to the house, we took one of the leftover Christmas cards, and both of us signed it. It had the Rantzows' address printed on the envelope. I wrote my name above it and sealed it with a silent wish.

When Iboya met Erik, she was clearly troubled. In my room she told me, "Piri, this young man is in love with you. You wrote that he was a friend. Have you been honest with him, about us leaving for America?"

"He knows, but we don't talk about it much."

"How do you feel about him?"

"I like him a lot; he has been a really good friend."

"I'm not so sure that you know the difference between friendship and love. I was concerned about you and Nore at times, afraid you might get involved with him. I even suspected that to be the motive of the Rantzows in bringing you here, but Nore loves you as a kid sister." Iboya paused. "I just don't understand you. You're only seventeen. You should not want to make a decision about your future now. Our papers will be ready for immigration in the spring."

"You're imagining things. Erik and I have never talked about making a commitment. It seems to me it is you and Rulle who are serious."

"He has applied for immigration papers. He is going to join us in America."

It was my turn to be surprised. "Have you told our relatives about this?"

"I told them about Rulle, but not that we were planning to get married. It would be too much of a shock. They think we are a couple of children. You remember what Auntie Simi wrote in one of her letters? 'Be sure to shampoo your hair, put on a clean dress, and act grown up when you go to see the consulate, so you will make a good impression.' " We both laughed.

"Who do they think has been looking after us all this time?" I asked.

Erik had taken some pictures of me from time to time, and I pulled them out and showed them to Iboya. "Don't send any of these to our relatives," she said, "especially not the one in the bathing suit and sunglasses. It might confuse them." Pointing to a framed enlargement of me that Erik had given Mama and Papa for Christmas, Iboya added, "You can send one of these; you look more innocent." It was sort of a posed portrait, taken in Erik's studio. Mama and Papa kept it on their dresser with all the other family photos.

It was hard to imagine what life would be like in America. How would we fit in? Our relatives said little about their way of life. My only images of America were from the movies—a shabby tenement in *A Tree Grows in Brooklyn* or glamorous Hollywood, with chauffeur-driven Rolls-Royces, diamonds, and mansions. From the few photos our relatives had sent us, I guessed they were somewhere in between the two.

Aunt Regina and Uncle Dave wrote that we would probably live with them in Bridgeport, Connecticut. They had recently sold a big house, after their four children had married, and moved into a three-bedroom ranch house. From the affidavits we received, we knew they owned a printing plant.

The most impressive photos came from Uncle Morris and Aunt Eva in Los Angeles. The house and car in the background looked plush. They had two daughters—in their mid-twenties, we guessed—who owned a bridal shop. "Perhaps we'll wind up in Los Angeles; it sounds more exciting from what Rulle tells me," Iboya explained.

The longer we speculated, the more apprehensive I felt about the whole thing. "Why would Rulle want to go to America and leave his whole family?"

"He was going to leave, even before he met me, and live in Australia. He is adventurous."

"I wouldn't want to go if I had a large family like he does. As long as you're planning to get married, why not stay here?"

"You don't really want to go, do you?"

"I'm not sure."

"Well, the main reason we are going is you," Iboya said.

I didn't bother to respond.

Erik's mother invited the Rantzows, Iboya, and me for dinner between Christmas and New Year's. I noticed Erik's father taking quite a fancy to my sister. She wore her wavy blond hair piled up high, with a twist in the back, and had applied powder and lipstick, put on high-heeled shoes and one of her American wool dresses. She was not a common sight in Astorp. But Erik's father, always so reserved, surprised me by spending most of the evening talking with her.

Erik's married sister, Rognil, was home from Stockholm for the holidays. I had heard so many affectionate stories about her that I felt as if I knew her, yet I was nervous about meeting her, afraid she was going to judge me. She was in the kitchen when we arrived, arranging a meat platter. Wiping her hands on a dish towel, she said, "Dear Piri, finally I get to meet you." She was almost as tall as Erik. They looked very much alike, but her personality was open and unrestrained. It almost clashed with her extraordinary beauty. Her eyes were a more vital green than Erik's, her chin-length smooth hair a warm brown, and her figure very feminine. I felt deflated in comparison. I wished I had worn a different dress, high-heeled shoes, even some of Iboya's lipstick. I went to the bathroom and took a long look at myself. "Definitely the little gypsy girl," I said aloud. I wet my brush and tried to tuck my hair behind my ears.

Rognil's husband, Nord, a bespectacled medical researcher, in contrast to his wife, was introverted. His well-worn green corduroy trousers suited him, unlike his sweater, which was brand-new, obviously a Christmas present. Their eight-year-old son, Lars, was a chip off the old block, including the wire-framed glasses. He looked like a midget scientist. He sat alone at a card table, engrossed in assembling a wooden puzzle.

After a couple of shot glasses of aquavit, Nord became almost animated in his conversation with Papa. It seemed that trains were one of his passions. He could not have picked a more informed expert in that field. Papa had spent thirty-three years of his life in locomotives. I would never have guessed that they had something in common, but as we were preparing to leave, they made a date to take Lars on a tour of the railroad yards. At the door, Rognil, who seemed to accept me, said to Erik, "You must bring Piri to Stockholm for a visit."

Back home, commenting on the evening, I said to Iboya, "You sure charmed Erik's father. Whatever were you talking about?"

"You and Erik mostly; he was trying to draw me out, to learn how you felt about the relationship and where Erik would fit into your life. You didn't tell me that he had been sick. They are still concerned about his health."

"What did you say to him?"

"I tried to explain that you are only seventeen, too young to make a decision about your future. He agreed that marriage is a big undertaking."

"You and Rulle are getting married," I pointed out.

"Rulle is twenty-nine, and I'm nineteen. Also, we are both of the same religion. I realize that living here among Christians, you have forgotten that you are Jewish."

Before she left the next day, Iboya gave me another lecture about not making any foolish decisions. "Remember, we are going to America!" It sounded like a threat.

11

It took me a while to feel relaxed again with Erik. Then Greta had a New Year's Eve party. When, after midnight, the couples started to drift into intimate corners of the house, Erik and I left. It was cold in the car and I sat close to him. "Where would you like to go?" he asked.

"Home." Driving was treacherous, with the snowdrifts making the roads almost invisible. With few cars in Astorp, there was no law about plowing.

After a couple of blocks, we had to abandon Charlie and walk the rest of the way. By the time we reached my house, we were half frozen. Mama crept down the stairs in her nightgown. I told her about having to leave the car. "Let Erik sleep in Nore's bed; he won't be coming home tonight." There was some grog, wine punch, left in the kitchen. We heated it and had several cupfuls to warm us up. It was only 1:00 a.m., early for New Year's Eve. We built up the fire in the living-room stove and put the radio on softly. I was no longer so cold, but I pulled my legs under me on the sofa and snuggled up to Erik. He hugged me, but remained deep in thought.

"You have been very quiet tonight," I commented. He shrugged his broad shoulders. My thoughts turned to Nore, Greta, and the other couples we had left behind.

They are making love, I thought. "Are you sorry you are with me instead of one of the Swedish girls?"

"No, I was wondering who you will be with next New Year's." Now I had no answer for him. We often spent long periods of time in silence. I had found it peaceful, but tonight our silence had an undercurrent.

Finally Erik spoke: "You must go and find out if you like it there. If you want me to come and join you, I could sell my share of the studio. I have no doubt about finding work in my field. Or if you want to come back, I'll send you passage. We don't have to live in Astorp. After America, it would be pretty dull. We could live in Stockholm. I could open a studio there; I have had some offers . . ." Erik moved away from me. "But these are all foolish words. You will never come back, and your relatives wouldn't want me . . ."

I could hardly believe what I heard. I wanted to say something reassuring, but could not think of anything worthy. Erik got up and paced the floor. He looked very mature for his twenty three years, and more appealing than I could ever remember. I felt undeserving of him. He offered so much and I had nothing to give in return. I felt that my destiny was not in my power; I was indebted to Iboya, and I wanted to join my relatives. Going to America had been part of my upbringing. Babi spoke of it as our salvation; my mother felt that it was the promised land. All her sisters and her brother lived there. The only reason she did not was because my grandmother would not leave her land.

Erik came back and sat down beside me. "I'm sorry I said all that. I just wanted you to know how I felt. I realize that you must do what is best for you and your sister. I understand your closeness, because I remember my own loneliness at the sanatorium."

I wished he was not always so understanding. It just

made me feel more guilty. I reached up and hugged his neck, pulling his face to mine. After a long kiss, I tried to convey my thoughts. "Erik, it is very difficult for me. I came to Astorp an orphan, to stay with strangers till I could go to America and live with relatives. The strangers became my family; now I think of my relatives in America as strangers. I feel secure and loved here, it would be very easy to stay. I also care for the Rantzows very much . . ." I stopped, knowing this was not what he was waiting to hear. "About us, I tried to keep you as a friend and not get involved emotionally. You are a good listener and you have great compassion, perhaps because of your own experiences, I don't know. But like the Rantzows, you broke down my defenses. I find myself vulnerable in your presence, and it upsets me. I don't want either one of us to get hurt."

"Have you ever been hurt before?" Erik asked.

"Yes, I have. I had my first romance in the ghetto before my fourteenth birthday. Not a very conducive atmosphere, but it made life more bearable."

"Have you ever heard from him?"

"No. Then I had a crush on someone at Visingso. He went to Palestine. Since then I've come to realize that I need affection and can't keep from getting involved."

"What about the man with the motorcycle?"

"You heard about him?" I asked.

"I saw him," Erik said. "He was quite a spectacle in Astorp. He stopped for directions in the village."

"I don't know about him. I never sorted him out."

"And Kaliu?"

"I just like the way he sings."

"So who were you hurt by?" Erik asked.

"The first two. Your turn."

"You'll be disappointed. There was only one, when I was in high school. She was at Gullan's party."

"Which one?"

"Her name is Ingrid. I danced with her once." I was overcome with jealousy. "She wore a black dress."

Now I remembered how she had looked at Erik—very intense, and she had made me feel the way Gullan made me feel, as if I did not belong there. "Did you love her?"

"I'm not sure, it was a long time ago, before I got sick. Then she went away to a university, and I to the sanatorium. She never wrote."

"Did you sleep with her?"

Erik laughed at me, and I got angry. "What difference does it make?"

"Then you did." I hated her with a passion!

"Piri, that was five years ago. I guess Gullan was trying to get us back together. She did not expect me to bring you. They are cousins."

I picked up my shoes and was ready to go upstairs, though I knew I would not sleep a wink. My blood was boiling.

"Piri, don't. She means nothing to me. I meant what I told you about us." As soon as Erik touched me, my anger vanished. I dropped my shoes and slipped my arms under his jacket, hugging him with all my strength. "We should quarrel more often," Erik whispered in my ear in a husky voice, and led me to the couch. He was grinning.

"I have warned you about my Hungarian temper," I teased.

Erik lifted off the back cushions of the couch to give us more room. He lay on his side and studied my face. I wondered if he could read my sudden hesitation. My passion was as strong as before, but I felt like a fraud. His white shirt was open, revealing dark short curls of hair. I reached over, opened several small buttons, and put my face against his chest. It was slightly moist, and I could feel his heart throb.

Erik turned onto his back, stroked my hair, and his heartbeat slowly relaxed. I kissed his chest indulgently to satisfy my craving. After a while it brought me contentment. "You are not a tiger, just a kitten," Erik said, kissing my face with affection. I kissed him back, in gratitude for his self-control. Eventually we arose and, carrying our shoes, tiptoed up the stairs to our rooms.

I woke late on New Year's Day. The glare of the sun on the snow was blinding in my room. I was afraid that Erik had long since gone to dig out his car. Wrapping my bathrobe around me, I pushed Nore's door ajar with caution, just in case. Erik was sleeping on his side, with his face toward the door. I stood and watched him for a moment. He sensed my presence and opened his sleepy eyes. He motioned for me to come closer. Looking behind me, I approached his bed slowly. He pulled me toward him and sniffed my neck, burying his face under my long hair, then kissed me on my mouth very gently. It felt more intimate than any other kiss. Slightly dazed, I straightened up and wondered why. Erik wanted another kiss, but I stole away to get dressed.

Mama fixed us Swedish pancakes and lingonberries for breakfast. She seemed exultant. "Did you and Papa have a nice New Year's Eve?" I asked.

"Very fine, Piri, all four of our sons called to wish us a healthy year." Then she and Erik exchanged a look of secrecy. What did it mean?

"Where is Papa?" I asked.

"I sent him with some food for Alfred Parson. He is too old to live alone. With all this snow, we hope he doesn't venture out. He should have married and had some children. It is a compensation in your old age."

Papa returned from Alfred Parson's with an empty basket before we were finished with breakfast. His cheeks were purple with cold. I jumped up to pour him some coffee.

"I passed your car," he said to Erik, sitting next to him. "It is half buried under snow. I asked some kids, out with their sleds, to dig it out for you and report back here when they have finished."

Erik blushed. "I could have done it myself."

"No need for you to be out getting chilled; besides, you can't drive the thing anyway. Even the trains are having a time of it. Only half a schedule at best. A good day to stay in and play dominoes—not even a paper to read." They took their coffee cups and left Mama and me in the kitchen. She closed the adjoining door to give us privacy and whispered, "Erik told me that he had proposed to you last night."

"When did he tell you that?"

"Just before you came down for breakfast."

I was perplexed. Mama watched my face and waited. "I did not realize that was a direct proposal."

"What did he say, *kära lilla Piri?*"

I repeated the words as well as I could remember them.

"That is a beautiful proposal," Mama exclaimed, "most noble and understanding."

"He did not say he loves me, even once, not ever."

Mama hugged me to her. "My dear child, he says that every time he looks at you. That is what Papa, Nore, and I like about him best. He is totally devoted to you. It is very apparent to everyone. His folks are aware of it, too, but they are worried about him. I called his mother this morning to tell her that you got home early and he had a good night's sleep."

"Mama, how do Erik's parents feel about me?"

"They are not opposed to you personally, I don't think, but like all parents, they would rather Erik had fallen in love with a local girl—less complications and conflicts. Also, they fear that you will leave for America and he will be hurt." Mama's last sentence implied a question.

"I don't know what is awaiting me."

"Can you tell your mama just one thing? How would you feel about Erik if there were no relatives in America?"

"I guess it would be different."

"That's all I wanted to hear," said Mama.

Before Nore went back to the military, he offered me some brotherly advice. "You'll never find a man better suited for you than Erik, so you better give it some serious consideration before you turn him down. And remember that we love you like our own." I suddenly realized that what I was missing was a girlfriend I could talk things over with. My diary was no longer sufficient.

Lisa, whom I saw from time to time, could not possibly comprehend the turmoil I was in. She had invited me skiing once recently. While she and her friends were gliding down a big hill, I stood with my aching feet, watching and envying their fun. Then Lisa asked me if I would like to borrow her boots and skis. I wasted no time in putting them on. With ski poles in hand, I gave myself a good starting push and let the momentum of the steep slope carry me down with the other skiers. At the bottom of the hill, I tried to halt by imitating their motions. I wound up with a twisted hip and crossed skis, embarrassed by the onlookers who came to my aid. Limping home, I was all too aware that I could not join Lisa and her friends' fun without the required training, any more than they could understand my problems without having had my experiences.

As for Nore's girlfriend, Greta, she was helpful in teaching me how to ride a bike and sew, but since she herself wanted so desperately to get married, she could not understand anyone else's hesitation.

So I decided to write to Dora in Stockholm. I poured out my heart to her in a long letter, confident that she would help me solve my troubles.

I was anxiously awaiting her reply when, one day in mid-February, Papa brought in the mail and handed me a letter from Italy. I stared at Lyral's name and address for a moment before opening the envelope. Three air-mail sheets of stationery covered with writing on both sides—I put all my concentration into it, absorbing the words like a starved man wolfing food into his mouth. And then I was overcome by frustration, realizing I could read only the first paragraph. Our common language had been "Concentration-Camp German." Lyral wrote in that dialect: "My happiness was very big to hear from you, because in my moving, I lost your old school address. Hope you can find a French translator, because I forgot, and refuse to remember, this bastard language." The rest was in a rush of French script. I ran to the phone to dial Erik's studio number. I remembered his telling me that during his stay in the sanatorium he had taken a correspondence course in French.

"How good is your French?" I asked. Silence. I could almost see that familiar puzzled look in his eyes. "I received a letter from Lyral, my French friend from the hospital. She is the one—"

"Yes, I remember."

"Well, I can't read it," I said. "She wrote it all in French."

"I'll come over with a dictionary tonight and try my best to help," Erik offered.

"I can't wait till then. Are you very busy? Could I come over now?"

"Yes, but I'm not sure how much I'll be able to interpret—it depends on how complex the letter is. My understanding of French is limited to books."

"If you could just tell me the essence, whether she found her child and André. I'm dying to know."

"Very well, come over," said Erik.

When I hung up the phone, I saw Papa and Mama waiting with curiosity for me to explain the dilemma of the letter. I felt a stab of guilt that I had not shared my past with them. "It is from a girl I met in Germany after the war. We were in the same ward, in a hospital."

Mama asked, "She lost a child?"

"I promise to tell you her story when I get back." I grabbed for my coat.

Mama handed me my boots. "You must put them on, and your hat and scarf as well." I did as I was told. On an impulse, I gave her a kiss, and a quick hug to Papa, who stood by silently.

The cold brisk walk was just what I needed to calm my anxiety. I could hear Lyral's melodious voice in the wind as I hurried through the snow-covered streets of Astorp. I remembered the words from her songs but did not know their meaning. If we should meet someday, we wouldn't be able to communicate, I realized with a start. Our vocabulary was very limited then, but we understood each other perfectly.

I had no trouble summoning up Lyral's face before me. There was something angelic about her appearance, but her will to survive for her child's sake was that of a Hercules. Though small and fragile, she seemed a maternal presence in the hospital, second only to Iboya. They cared for me like nurses, taking shifts.

By the time I reached the studio, my compassion for Lyral was overflowing. The bell announced my entrance and Erik came to greet me from the darkroom. I extended the crumpled letter. He sat down and I watched him, trying to judge from his expression the contents of the letter. He glanced up at me after the first page. "I think it's best if I read it through first. Let me grasp the main points."

"Can you understand her writing?"

"I'm getting most of it better than I thought." Erik read and reread, nodding his head. At last he seemed ready. "Basically, she had a hard time looking after her mother, who had a heart ailment, till her mother died. Then she continued her search for her daughter, Irma. She had some clues that she pursued; that is why she went to Italy. She narrowed it down to a convent orphanage, through some man who kept the child for a while and then left her with the nuns there. But the convent was disbanded during the war, and the orphans were dispersed. However, she feels very hopeful that the child is alive. Meanwhile, she is staying with this man, and he has been very helpful in pursuing the search with her. She says that he, too, loves her little girl, and since he was the last one to see her, the child would probably remember him. He has paintings of her. That is how Lyral found him, through a portrait he painted of Irma, in Paris."

I was more than puzzled. "Who is this man?"

"It seems he is an artist, and the child was sent to him from Paris by his sister, who was a friend of Lyral's mother. I don't know if this whole thing makes sense to you."

"It is a complicated letter."

"Yes, and also she was very excited when she wrote it. If only I were more fluent in my French. Why don't you leave the letter with me, and I'll make a translation of it with my French dictionary. I'll call you later and let you know how I'm doing." Erik gave me a kiss and led me through the door. The cold air hit me full force. I did not realize that I had been sitting in the studio all bundled up.

Mama was waiting with hot coffee. "Was it good news?"

"I'm not sure. Erik will read it more carefully and call me."

"You promised to tell me about this friend and her child."

I could see Mama's anguish as I told her a little about Lyral's problems; it was so obviously affecting her that I was scared. "Mama, I don't think this is a good idea."

"Then just tell me about yourself. What actually was your sickness?"

"But I have told you many times. You know, my frozen feet, malnutrition, I had a fever . . ."

"But what did the doctors call it?" she asked.

"Typhoid. We were all sick."

"Dear little Piri, you always brush me aside. We have so little knowledge about you."

Lyral's letter had opened up all the questions I had been trying to avoid. "Mama, what would you like to know?"

"Well, we have heard all sorts of stories . . . Were you ever hurt by one of those German soldiers?"

When I had first come to Astorp, I still had frequent nightmares. Mama would come and sit on my bed and ask if I wanted to tell her about it. I never did. But now I felt cornered. "Once or twice I was beaten."

"Did any of them bother you . . ." She could not go on, but it was not difficult to read her question clearly.

"Mama, Lyral's child was not from a German. Lyral is Christian; she was not in our camp. The father is a Frenchman." I realized then that André had not even been mentioned in Lyral's letter.

Mama was still waiting to hear about me. "Just once

I was grabbed by an SS man. This was when I worked in the kitchen in Christianstadt and I was sent to take food up to a guard in one of the lookout towers. I first thought he was being friendly. He asked me questions about my home and my family while he was eating his lunch. I sat down on the threshold of the tower with my feet resting on the last step, so I was not inside the cubicle with him. I was just waiting for him to finish so I could take back the dishes, when he got up with a mouthful of food and came toward me. I did not like the look in his eyes as he reached down to catch me. I struggled, holding on to the frame of the door, and managed to give him a shove back into the tower with my foot. Then I ran down the steps. Well, I ran down half of them and fell the rest of the way. He yelled for me to come back for the lunch pail, but I just kept running. The two guards at the gate gave me a good looking-over. I was bleeding from my mouth, and had skinned my shins, and the front of my gray uniform was torn. 'I fell and cut my mouth,' I offered as a plea of mercy to them, so they would let me pass. After a sly grin, one of them opened the gate."

While relating the incident to Mama, I realized that this was the first time I had ever told anyone.

"What happened when you got back to the kitchen?" Mama asked.

"Frau Hoffman and Frau Rubichack, the two older ladies who worked as chefs, took care of me," I replied.

"Did they ever send you back to the tower guards after that?"

"No, they picked another girl."

"Is that when you lost your front tooth?"

I had tried not to think about my missing tooth; I even hoped that by now it wasn't noticeable. Two other teeth had moved over, closing in half the space. I was really conscious of it only when I looked in the mirror, wondering how a man like Erik could find me attractive, or when I was posing for a photo. Now that Mama brought it up, I stuck my tongue into the space. "Did you ever see that German again?" she asked.

"Yes, once, when we were to have an inspection of the kitchen. I was standing on a chair, cleaning one of the huge gas cauldrons, scraping the food off its sides, and I saw him come into the kitchen. I bent my head and leaned over so he would not recognize me. He came up behind me, picked my feet off the chair, and threw me in. Luckily the gas was turned low, just enough for the dishwater to remain warm. I was able to scramble out without being scalded. When I looked up, dripping wet and covered with food particles, I saw him watching me from the door with a sick look of satisfaction on his face."

Erik's laborious translation of Lyral's letter had little more than additional details, but I appreciated his taking the trouble. Now I was able to send it to Iboya, knowing she, too, would be thrilled to hear from Lyral again.

12

In March, Erik got an assignment for a job in Stockholm through his sister. He invited me to come along. I jumped at the chance, not only because I wanted so much to see the capital, but also because it would give me a chance to visit Dora and Hershi. I needed more than ever to speak with Dora. She had answered my long letter, saying that I relied too much on Iboya. "If you did not have a sister," she wrote, "you would have to use your own judgment. Also, if you reread your letter, I'm surprised that you did not see the obvious, that you don't express your feelings toward Erik as love. Instead of asking me what I think, why don't you ask yourself how you feel. You will be eighteen in a couple of months. You can't be dependent on Iboya forever." As usual, Dora spoke to the point.

I did do some thinking about my dependency on Iboya. In anything I ever wanted to do, I first considered what Iboya would think and how it would affect her. Perhaps I used my loyalty as an excuse. I had always let her manage what little money we had. I let her take care of the main correspondence with the relatives in America and with our sister, Etu; and make the arrangements for our immigration visas. Was I doing this so I would not have to take the responsibility? The answer I came up with in my soul searching was her hurt look on the few minor occasions when I had disobeyed her. "Don't you trust that I only want the best for you?" I did not see a way of changing our relationship without jeopardizing our closeness, and I decided that our closeness was more important than anything else, since we had only each other.

As for Erik, how was I to know if I was really "in love"? I had been certain that I was in love with Henri in the ghetto. And what about David at school, I asked myself. Had I loved him? If I did, how could I have gotten over it and now love Erik? Could I get over loving Erik? I was as confused as when I had written the letter to Dora. In person, I was hoping, she would be able to help me.

We arrived in Stockholm in the middle of the month. The city was cast in a twilight of grays, with yellow flickering lights outlining the large buildings and guiding our way. I was overwhelmed by its magnitude. I had never seen Budapest or any other capital before, so I was not prepared for its majesty. It reduced the people to midgets in comparison.

Erik's brother-in-law, Nord, picked us up at the train station and, for my benefit, pointed out the landmarks as we drove through broad streets with incredible and varied architecture. It all looked so modern, yet Nord was telling me it dated back to the thirteenth century—"in just five years, Stockholm will celebrate its seven hundredth anniversary," he said. "The old part of the city was built and ruled by the Danes; it did not become Sweden's capital until the seventeenth century. Since then we have had our own monarch. Erik must take you around to see Storkyrka—the church with the statue of St. George and the Dragon—and the Riddarholm Church. Also Djurgarden Park, our pleasure resort; it has both a zoo and a large open-air museum. The buildings of the museum represent different periods of Sweden."

"My friend Dora, who lives here," I said, "sent me some postcards—one of Town Hall with the three golden crowns, one of a palace, and one of a seaport. I would especially like to see that palace."

Erik, who had been in one of his meditative moods, declared, "Then you shall see it, of course! Tomorrow I will be busy most of the morning making arrangements for Saturday's shooting, but we have all of Sunday, and possibly Monday as well."

Nord and Rognil lived in one of Stockholm's suburbs. We turned a corner near a huge shopping area. It had dozens of stores confined in one place, more than all the stores on Main Street in Beregszász. Rognil and Lars were waiting for us in the driveway. Even preoccupied, Lars seemed delighted to see us. They lived in a two-bedroom house furnished in Swedish modern, with several needlecraft wall hangings, earthenware pottery, and colored glass. It looked open and cheerful. Only the most up-to-date couples in Astorp decorated this way. Again I felt out of place. I did bring my American clothes, but they were a dressy assortment. Rognil's outfit was more relaxed; it suited the surroundings. I freshened up and changed to a fuchsia silk blouse and dared a bit of pink lipstick. When I came back to the living room, Erik gave me a surprised but approving look. "What a marvelous color for your dark hair," Rognil commented, as she served us some sherry.

I called Dora. Her voice was high-pitched with excitement. She had a million plans for us. "I can't wait to meet Erik; can you come for dinner tomorrow?"

"I'll check and let you know when I see you in the morning."

"Good. I have a goulash and things all prepared."

I was tired from the trip yet exhilarated, and the sherry gave me the sensation of a holiday. After a leisurely dinner, Rognil helped me make up the studio couch in Lars's room. Erik was to sleep on the living-room sofa. "We will be getting up early, but you two can sleep till I get back from the market," Rognil told us before retiring.

In the morning, Rognil drove Lars to school and dropped Nord off at his office so Erik could have the car. I was being lazy and waited to get up till after they left. Also, there was only one bathroom, so I thought it would be more convenient if we did not all try to wash at the same time. Opening my eyes, I stretched and looked out the window above my head. I still could not believe that I was actually in Stockholm. My door opened, and there was Erik in his bathrobe, carrying a tray. On it was hot chocolate topped with whipped cream, and sweet buns. I felt like a princess. "For me?"

"Yes, but first you must give me a kiss. Remember when I slept in Nore's room on New Year's Eve? You came in while I was still in bed and gave me a kiss. Last night, thinking about it and knowing that you were in the next room kept me up half the night." He put the tray down on Lars's desk and sat down on my bed. By the time Erik slipped his arms about me, I could hardly catch my breath. Our embrace was too passionate—I made him stop, wishing my life wasn't so complicated.

Later in the car, driving me to Dora's, Erik was quiet. I was lost in the view. In spite of the daylight, Stockholm retained its sober grays. The massive stone-and-glass buildings were austere, the trees still in their winter bareness. The sun, eclipsed by moving clouds, occasionally cast rays over a patch of the city, like a searchlight. The only spots of color were the pedestrians. There was a constant stream of cars and buses; everyone seemed to be on the move. "So many people in Stockholm," I commented.

"Most of them are underground," Erik said casually. I was jolted. "They're building underground trains all through Stockholm," he added. I burst out laughing in relief. He joined me and squeezed my hand.

"Are you upset with me because of this morning?" I asked.

"No."

"You should be, it was cruel of me. I wanted to. That good-morning kiss in Nore's room . . . it was special for me, too. I have never felt like that. Never!" I looked at him for the first time since he had left my room, and there was a pleased smile on his face.

"I'm very glad of that," Erik said. "Don't forget to call me at Rognil's around 5:30 p.m. I should be there by then."

"What about dinner?"

"Insist they let me take them out. It would really be much simpler, and I would like to do that."

When we pulled up to Dora's building, Dora was outside and so ecstatic that she was reaching for the door before the car came to a full stop. Erik stood watching us hug and chatter from a few steps away. I brought him over and made the introductions. Erik towered over Dora. Looking up with her big blue eyes, she said after what seemed a long minute, "It is so good to meet you."

Erik held her gaze. "I have also been looking forward to it. Now, you two have a lot to catch up on. I'll see you for dinner."

Before the car was in motion, Dora and I were talking at the same time. We walked up four old flights of stairs and entered a small apartment. The furniture was a mixture from secondhand shops, but cozy. Fresh flowers were on the coffee table, plants on the windowsills, and the aroma of a cake baking sweetened the air. We took off our coats and looked each other over. Dora seemed half the size she had been the last time I saw her. "You got so small."

"And you have filled out—my God, you are a real woman!" As we embraced, I was sure she had shrunk. We had been the same size. "He is so good-looking and charming. You are a fool if you let this man get away."

"You don't even know him," I said.

"From what you have told me and what I have just seen, he is a dream. After what you have been through, to get a chance for a man like him . . . What is the problem?"

"I told you."

Dora led me to the couch and lit a cigarette. "I can't believe you are not in love with him."

"I guess I'm just dumb but I don't know what I feel," I said. "Anyway, let's leave that for later. Tell me about you and Hershi."

"We are planning to get married as soon as possible. We are determined to pay off our debts and fix up the apartment. Maybe we are foolish to wait, but by then, Hershi will be more relaxed. I don't want him to feel pressured again. You know how he is . . ."

"Is he working today?"

"Only till 4:00 P.M. He is doing something for Pali."

"Pali—I thought you were not friendly."

"It just did not work—staying mad, I mean. Hershi feels indebted to him. He always will. You know, Pali played big brother to him and saved his life. I have to accept it." She drew on her cigarette. "Pali has come around quite a bit; he doesn't meddle between us anymore. He offered Hershi a partnership in his bakery, but I'm afraid that would bring them too close again."

"Does Pali own a bakery?" I asked. "He is amazing."

"He bought somebody out. I don't know all the details, but according to Hershi, it will be a big success. He calls it the Hungarian Pastry Shop. He knows you are in town and wants us to meet him for a drink later."

"He sure has a thick skin, wanting to see me after I would not accept his registered letters."

"He said you are the little girl from his past, but is he in for a shock. You can't imagine how different you look."

"They are very good to me, my Swedish family," I said. "I have a home, I belong. I don't suffer from those stomach cramps anymore. I sleep through the night without nightmares—occasionally I have them, but I guess that is natural."

"God," said Dora, "I remember the one you used to have about not being able to find your house. You would wake up in a cold sweat."

"I finally figured out what it was. I used to compose letters in my mind to my friend Ica Molnar while lying in bed in Visingso, promising myself to write them down in the morning. I was not sure how much to tell her. I was worried about what questions she might ask, what she would tell me had happened to Beregszász. In my dream, I would go home to see for myself, and I could not remember our address. I would be walking in a maze of blocks, all in a panic, passing our Christian neighbors, but I would be ashamed to ask any of them, 'Do you remember where the Davidowitz family used to live?' Then after Etu wrote about what happened, I decided not to write to Ica anymore. And the dreams stopped." I paused. "Is it not silly for us to be wasting our time on old dreams?"

"You are right," Dora said. "Let me just take the cake out of the oven, then we had better go."

"But Erik insists he wants to take us out to a restaurant, so we can sit and get to know each other. Who knows, we might wind up living in Stockholm and being neighbors."

"God, you are mixed up!"

I proceeded to tell Dora about New Year's Day and this morning. When I finished, she seemed disappointed. "What you have described are sexual feelings, not love."

"If it is not love, which is what I thought it was, then I must ask you, is it all right and feminine for me to have such a need?"

Dora burst out laughing, but quickly stifled it. "I'm sorry, but I just can't believe your innocence. It is perfectly normal for a woman to have desires. We are not so different from men. Our culture has set two different standards for us, but our bodies send out the same signals."

"Then how did you know that you were in love with Hershi?"

"I guess my first attraction to him was physical; I liked the way he looked, especially his red hair. And from the moment I met him on the boat, I sensed in him a certain need for companionship. I recognized it because I was lonely, too. Even as a little girl, because my parents were separated and I was so dependent on my mother, I remember following her around like a little puppy. So I understand Hershi's bond to Pali. Our relationship is built on understanding. Hershi and I have been very honest with each other from the beginning. The pregnancy was an unfortunate accident, but it wasn't his fault. He does not talk about it, but he has tried to make up for it, shielding and supporting me during all other crises. We'll just have to try to live with it, along with the rest of our past. We have a private saying between us: 'A look back and a step forward.' " All the while Dora spoke, her eyes were bathed with adoration. Though she did not explain love tangibly, she demonstrated it. Maybe love cannot be defined, I thought, because it means different things to different couples.

"Take Ida, for instance," Dora was saying.

"Ida?"

"Yes, I see her occasionally and she always remembers to ask about you, but I did not tell her that you were coming to Stockholm. I was too selfish and wanted you to myself."

"How is Ida? Is she happy with her marriage and becoming a Swede?"

"She has been finding out that it isn't quite so simple to turn into someone you're not. Her Orthodox roots nag at her." I shook my head in sympathy. "But that is only part of her problem. Ida married this man to run away from her and her sister's past, and she is guilt-ridden. Her husband, guessing that her unhappiness comes from being a stranger in a strange land, is trying to make up for it by showering her with kindness. His attentiveness makes her feel even more deceitful, so she in turn is the most dedicated wife and mother. They take turns being each other's slave. It won't work, unless Ida makes a confession."

"What is the big dark secret? I always suspected there was something strange about her sister. She was so introverted and detached. At first I thought she was conceited because of her looks, but I realized she was hardly aware of it."

"I started to tell you about it once, but Magda was there, and also Iboya. Ida unburdened herself to me on the day she found out that her sister was going to be married. Up to that time, Ida was talking about becoming a Swede as if she were learning a part for a play. Well, it seems that the two sisters were in a work camp, where they came into daily contact with political prisoners. These men were allowed to receive mail and parcels from home. The only thing they lacked was female companionship. So they started flirting with the best-looking women. Now, you know Ida's sister must have been the most beautiful there. Or anywhere. At first she was very flattered by the attention. She accepted the delicacies of preserved meats, fish, crackers, and chocolate, giving most of them to Ida, never realizing where it would all lead. They even managed to get her silk stockings, lace underwear, and lipstick. Then, as with all favors and gifts, she had to reciprocate. Before long she was intimately involved with several of the male prisoners. That came to an abrupt end the winter the Russians approached their camp. Ida and her sister, along with all the other women, were put on a death march by German soldiers, forced to walk aimlessly. The prisoners were dropping like bundles of rags by the roadside. The soldiers would grant them one bullet apiece and leave them to the elements. Ida was failing, and it looked as if she would be next. Ida's sister took out her lipstick and rouged her cheeks and lips, making herself as alluring as possible under such circumstances. She soon attracted advances from the soldiers.

"When they stopped at a farm for the night, the prisoners, if lucky, would be sheltered in the barn with the animals and given a potato or turnip in the morning. The soldiers would take the best part of the house, often sending the farmers off to their kin after they had prepared a good meal for them. Then Ida's sister would be let into the house with two other favored young women. They got to take warm baths and stay part of the night, till the soldiers fell into drunken slumber. Thus Ida's sister managed to continue to sneak food to Ida and sometimes a few others. Nobody did any condemning, unless in anger for not being included in the favors. But as soon as the war was over, they started to call her a whore. I think the reason Ida and her sister were put on the boat to Sweden with us Hungarians was to save them from their *landsmen.*"

"Dora," I said, "I'm not sure what all this has to do with love."

"What I'm saying, Piri, is that Ida's marriage won't work unless she is honest about her past with her husband. That's what love is all about. As for you, you refuse to be honest even with yourself. Make up your mind, and if you're going to America, the sooner you tell Erik, the better."

There was one complication in my relationship with Erik that I could not discuss with Dora. I felt that she, being a Budapesti and not having been brought up the way I was, would not understand my conscience asking me what did I survive for if I did not remain a Jew?

It was noon by the time we left Dora's apartment. The streets were immaculately clean. The sun filtered down in the courtyards dividing the buildings. Swelling buds on the trees were ready to burst and unravel into leaves at the stroke of spring. My winter coat became a burden during our brisk walk. Dora, like Nord, was giving me a tour, pointing out the landmarks, but she lacked his enthusiasm.

When I showed my enchantment with Stockholm, Dora countered, "Someday you must see Budapest. It has much more charm. I wish I could take you for lunch to one of the cafés on Andrassy Ut, or along the Danube to listen to violins while we eat *palacsinta* and drink *habos kávé.* Instead, I'll take you to Saltsjobaden. It's too early for the beaches, but we can go to one of the islands and watch the ships."

We sat in a restaurant with a pretty view of the many small islands that lie in Saltsjobaden. I fantasized sitting there with Erik someday, after we were married. The restaurant was filled with couples looking out as ships, boats, and barges sailed by. The waitress brought our food, and I realized how hungry I was. I had never eaten the sweet rolls Erik had brought me on the tray.

"This omelet is too runny," Dora called to the waitress.

"And I would like some lemon for my tea," I said. Our eyes met, and we laughed at our grand elegance. It does not take long to get used to being spoiled.

By the time we met Hershi and Pali for a drink at four in the afternoon, we were exhausted from an afternoon of sightseeing; our feet were aching, and our throats were sore from constant conversation. Somehow, rising above it all, I felt elated. But the thought of facing Pali disheartened me.

"Oh, come on, we can't deny the poor fool his pleasure," said Dora, reaching for the heavy glass door. "It will be all over in an hour, then we can go meet your prince, Erik. I'm really glad I won't have to fix dinner, you wore me out." I spotted Pali as soon as we entered. He sat in a booth facing the door. He jumped up to greet me, and planted a wet kiss on each of my cheeks. He was freshly shaved and reeked of cologne. As he helped me off with my coat, his black eyes penetrated my dress. I felt naked.

"How you have grown up, young lady! The country life agrees with you." Hershi seemed uneasy as he embraced me, as though not sure whether I had forgiven him about Dora and the baby. I gave him an extra squeeze to assure him that I held no grudge.

When Pali asked "What is your preference," I really wanted a glass of water, but I asked for wine just to show off. It was a mistake. I drank it fast to quench my thirst, and it went straight to my head. I made an effort to look alert, but Dora and Hershi seemed twenty feet away from me. Yet Pali's prying questions and boasting seemed deafening.

"You can't leave Stockholm without seeing my bakery. These poor Swedes will find out how real bread should taste, not like the heavy coarse stuff they have been feeding on. We'll also have crèmes, tarts, and strudels filled with nuts, cheese, and poppy seeds. I have found a first-rate baker with Budapest experience. Hershi can be the manager, but we still need Dora's approval." Hershi cast an apologetic look at Dora. Pali picked it up. "Why am I raving on like this? I guess I'm just overexcited to see my little girlfriend grown into an elegant young lady. It is hard to believe a flower blooming—" Pali cut the sentence short and downed his drink. "It is a damn miracle, you and Hershi both."

Dora looked at Hershi and said softly, "A look back, a step forward."

To change the mood, Pali asked me, "How is Iboya these days?"

"She is dating a very nice man. I think they are planning to get married."

"I'm happy she has finally come around to thinking of herself. I hope you are appreciative of how she devoted herself to you."

I was furious with Pali for making me feel like a child. Dora said, "Pali, don't you think that people do things out of a personal need, that if they did not want the responsibility of caring for another person, they would not choose to?"

"How would you know, you were always an only child." Pali controlled his voice. "I had three sisters and a brother. You never needed to look after anyone."

"Having someone to care for is as important as having someone care for you," Dora said.

"Strange to hear it coming from you, Dora, an *einer allein*."

"I did not survive alone. My mother was with me for the first five months in Auschwitz, giving me half her daily rations, and after that her spirit stayed with me."

The anger in Pali's face was replaced with admiration. "You're a strong little woman, to have made it on your own. I'm not as independent. I need your man to motivate me. Are you going to let him be my partner and manager?" Dora took a deep breath, reached across the table, and shook hands with Pali.

The bakery was just down the street, next to numerous other storefronts. In it were carpenters and electricians working overtime. Pali looked out of place, leading us through the dust-covered store in his immaculate suit and polished shoes. He drew shelves and work counters in space, explaining the layout of the shop.

After another round of hugs and kisses, he put us in a taxi and we waved to his vanishing silhouette. "That wasn't so bad, and I got to see the bakery. Pretty impressive!" Dora said to Hershi. Then, looking me over, she commented sarcastically, "He still has not lost his touch with you."

"Actually, I feel sorry for him."

"Oh, he'll be all right; he is completely entranced by this project, and I think he is developing real affection for Katica. I would not be surprised if they beat us to the altar."

My expression must have mirrored my astonishment, for Hershi gave Dora a questioning look.

"I did not tell Piri, we had so much to talk about," Dora said. "Pali has been living with this girl. She was born in Sweden, but has a Hungarian father."

I felt relief at the prospect of Pali having a wife. "What is she like?"

"Real pretty, smallish, blond, with brown eyes. Best of all, she looks up to Pali to the point of worship. I think she could replace his need for both you and Hershi."

I was glad that we got to the restaurant before Erik. It gave me a chance to freshen up and also ask Dora why she had kept Katica a secret. "I was so sure he would bring her to show off to you that I did not want to influence your opinion of her. She came into the picture while I was away at the home . . . they were a jolly threesome while I carried the world on my shoulders. She is a friend of Hershi's cousin. That is how they met her. I think Hershi's aunt was trying to have Hershi fall for her, but Katica surprised everyone. To her, Pali is the champion survivor. I'm very sorry you did not get to see her drool over him. You would have found it shocking." I could detect something unsaid in Dora's story, some sort of jealousy, but I could not grasp its reason.

Erik looked tired when he came in, but he soon perked up. He was impressed by Hershi's Swedish. "How did you manage to learn our difficult language so fluently?"

"He works at it," said Dora proudly.

"I enjoy the challenge," Hershi explained. "Hungarians are known to be poor at learning foreign languages. I would like to disprove the myth."

"Piri unfortunately picked up the Skane accent in Astorp. It is very amusing and charming, of course, but it would be difficult to unlearn."

"Astorp did more than alter her speech; she developed into a woman," said Hershi matter-of-factly. Dora and I looked at each other and giggled like kids, surprised that he would notice.

As the evening went on, I was amazed to discover how similar Hershi and Erik were. Both of them expressed themselves in minimal words, yet nothing passed them by.

On our second trip to the ladies' room, Dora took my arm. "Listen, Piri. I was not only observing Erik tonight, I was also watching you. Your whole personality changes in his presence. He makes you come alive. I think you're in love with him, but you're just afraid to admit it." I didn't say anything.

After we dropped Hershi and Dora off, Erik drove around till we came to the Gota Canal, which connects Stockholm with Göteborg. We sat and looked out over the water. A multitude of lights were reflected in its dark surface. In the distance we could see the outline of a ship. I remembered the boat that brought me from Germany to Sweden. It seemed such a long time ago.

"What are you thinking about?" Erik asked.

"About us."

"Are they happy thoughts?"

"Yes. I love being here with you."

"Do you? Yet you looked so sad," Erik whispered, taking me in his arms.

Sunday we all had breakfast together; then Erik and I took the underground and the ferry to Djurgarden Park. We strolled arm in arm, immersed in the scenic beauty. Erik enjoyed my recognizing various trees and shrubbery. He had no knowledge of them.

"It is from my early summers spent at my grandmother's farm," I told him.

"No, it is from your love of nature. I'm a country boy, but I took no interest in such things."

At the zoo, we fed the animals and acted like children. Erik had to teach me some of their names in Swedish. I was familiar with farm animals, but I could only identify most of the zoo creatures from storybooks. The camels, llamas, and elephants overwhelmed me—I was afraid to hold my hand to their hungry mouths. Erik teased me, "And I thought you were so tough." We watched glass being blown in the glassmaker's house. Erik explained the techniques, then bought me an amber glass lizard as a souvenir, making me feel like a little girl at a fair.

Whatever we did was a new experience. I felt totally carefree, overcome with the joy of being alive. Erik must have sensed my mood, and surprised me by casting away his usual reserve. Skipping down a narrow path, he jumped up to touch a high branch over his head. He picked me up and stood me on top of a bench, then grabbed me around the waist and twirled me till I was dizzy. I could hardly believe this lightheartedness and encouraged him by running off and hiding behind the fat trunk of a tree. Pretending he did not see me, Erik ran past. Soon we were both on a bench, panting with exhaustion and laughter.

"I have not done this since school," Erik said wistfully.

"I wish I had known you then."

"You would not have liked me. Before I got sick, I was wild; I would have scared you off."

"Still, I could have known you longer." As soon as the words were out, I knew I had said the wrong thing, but it was too late.

Erik's eyes turned serious. "Longer than . . . ?"

All I could say was "I'm sorry."

The sun was fading, there was a cold wind, and I noticed that the park was almost deserted. Sunday was drawing to an end. Erik looked at his watch; we had promised Rognil to be back by four for dinner. "We better get going," he said.

The ride back on the underground was long and listless. Rognil's home, with warm light and bright colors, was a welcome sight. Nord poured us refreshments, and by the time we were seated at dinner, we felt hungry and restored.

We spent Monday sightseeing. The most remarkable thing about Stockholm was the contrast of the ancient with slick, modern commercial buildings. Our last stop was the PUB department store, to buy some gifts for our families. I was just as astounded standing in the middle of a floor of merchandise as I was by the splendor of the Riddarholm Church. Here people were calmly going up and down moving stairs, as if it was the most ordinary thing to do. I could hardly concentrate on our purchases, seeing so many riches under one roof where people could choose and buy with no restraint but their budget. Erik was a bit annoyed by my lack of help in making selections. How could I explain to him the world of poverty and hunger that my mind was making an involuntary comparison with?

As I came down one of the escalators, my eyes were drawn to a display of fuzzy slippers. I slipped my hands into a pair, wishing Mother could have them, remembering what little luxury she had had. A saleslady in a professional voice asked, "Froken, would you like to purchase those slippers?"

"Yes, I would" came my prompt reply.

When I paid for them at the register, Erik joined me. "Good, at least you bought your mama a present," he commented encouragingly. I did not reply.

By the time we were seated on the train bound for Astorp, we were worn out. I dozed on and off most of the trip, rocked by the train and settled in Erik's arms.

13

Papa came home at midday on Tuesday in his civilian clothes, looking older than when I had left for Stockholm. He had his right arm in a sling. At first I thought he had fallen, but Mama explained that he had been bothered again by the same pain he had suffered all winter, and finally she had persuaded him to see Dr. Abrahamson. An X-ray revealed a deposit of calcium. "Now they have to find a way to dissolve it," Mama said.

I recalled Papa having discomfort in taking off the tight-fitting jacket of his railroad uniform. "I'm just getting old," he would say as he tried to rotate his shoulder in an effort to loosen up the joint. I would massage it and he would grimace but tell me, "Go on, it feels good."

"Piri, the doctor offered the same treatment you did," Mama said. "He is going to send a professional masseuse to the house three times a week."

During the evenings after that, I observed the lady in white kneading Papa's shoulderblade with her strong hands, then pounding it till blood rushed to the area, making it red and blotchy. I would repeat the treatment on alternate days, imitating her technique. In a week's time Papa went back to work, but the idea of his not being fit bothered me. He had never missed a day's work since I had come to live there.

Then there was a long letter from Iboya, telling me that we must have copies of our new birth certificates ready by the end of April for our affidavits. The two Hollander sisters would act as witnesses. "It had to be two people who could verify our true age, since we have no original proof of birth. When you come for Passover, we'll go visit them and have them sign at a notary's."

I could hardly believe that Erik and I had been away only four days and so much had taken place in our absence. I felt agitated and cross; I would get upset with Erik over the slightest disagreement and start a quarrel.

Mama tried to console me, blaming my irritability on my being premenstrual, but when it lasted past the time, she suggested I go along with Papa on his next visit to Dr. Abrahamson. Papa was glad to have the company. He felt uneasy with doctors.

While Papa was receiving his treatment in one room, I got a physical examination in the other. Dr. Abrahamson was a soft-spoken, fatherly type. He took his time with the exam and asked many questions about my camp experiences and my life in Astorp. Considering his gentle manner, he was surprisingly personal.

Finally he put away his instruments. "What has been troubling you? Your mama"—Dr. Abrahamson pronounced "mama" as a question—"tells me you have been irritable lately. What do you think caused your change of behavior?"

I told him of my concern over Papa's bursitis and about my trip to America being imminent—September or October most likely.

"Don't you want to go and be with your family?"

You don't understand, either, I thought, but tried to be polite. "It is hard to explain, but the Rantzows *are* my family. They treat me like their own daughter. And now Papa is sick, and Mama is not well, either."

"He is not sick, he will be fine."

"But they will miss me," I said.

The doctor nodded. "And what about your sister?"

"She wants to go, but you see, it is different with her. She always thought of Sweden as a stopover, and her boyfriend is going to follow us."

"Would you want Erik to follow you?"

"I'm not sure. He is Christian; I don't think my family would approve of him . . ."

"You know what I think, Piri? I think you are very young and you have missed a whole lot. In America, you can have a fresh start. You might want to go to school; you are a bright young woman . . . you must give yourself an opportunity to find out what you have missed. It is very noble of you to feel loyalty to the Rantzows; they deserve a lot of credit, but they have their own children. Erik, too, will get over it. The two of you were drawn together because of both of your experiences, but there are many differences between you. You are leaning on each other, but you must not let him stand in your way. And frankly, I don't think you would be the best choice for him, either. He belongs with his own kind." Dr. Abrahamson gave me a prescription and walked me through the door. He asked me to come talk to him anytime I felt like it, but I never did.

I found Papa walking around in the doctor's garden, puffing on his pipe. He looked at me anxiously. "What did he find wrong?"

"Not a thing. He gave me this prescription for some pills to calm my nerves, but said it was just the change in having gone to Stockholm. Maybe it's spring fever. Look, Papa, there are some crocuses pushing through the ground. Soon there will be color everywhere. I can smell it in the air."

"What can you smell?"

"Spring, Papa, it is just around the corner."

He shook his head, in the way he usually did when Mama and I were engaged in women's talk.

Two weeks later, when the invitation arrived from Rulle's mother, both Papa and I were back to feeling fit and cheerful.

Spring was very much apparent as I arrived at the Slobodkins' for Passover. The flower shops were bursting. Iboya and I bought a bouquet for the Passover table. Rulle's sisters, Ulla and Sonya, were amused with my Skane dialect to the point that it bothered me. They were very good-natured about it, but I guess I was just too sensitive about anything pertaining to Astorp. The life here was strikingly different—it was citified and luxurious. My dear papa would have felt out of place. Somehow I felt out of place myself.

We took tea in the salon, on Rosenthal china, picking up tiny sugar lumps with delicate sterling tongs. Eating a small pastry in six bites while Rulle played classical music on the piano, Iboya amazingly seemed born to this life. After tea, they all played bridge and sipped Vichy water. I was back to being the little gypsy girl again.

The seder dinner was full of nostalgia for me. I sat with the Slobodkin family and their guests, but in my thoughts I was back in Komjaty. Iboya kicked my foot under the table, wearing much the same expression as Mother, to bring me out of my fantasy world. The older she got, the more she resembled Mother, not only in looks, but also in mannerisms. It put her at a great advantage; I could never get really mad at her. At least the color of their eyes was different.

When the meal was finished, I was glad to be able to get up and move about. My head felt heavy and dazed by all my memories. Perhaps the reason I felt so content at the Rantzows' was that there was so little similarity there to my former life. Maybe Dr. Abrahamson was right that Erik and I were using each other as a crutch, rather than face reality. I had given the doctor's words a lot of thought. I also puzzled over why he had chosen to live in Astorp. As far as I knew, he was the only Jew who had settled there. I had found out that his wife was Christian, but nobody seemed to know any more than that about him.

The next day Iboya and I went to visit the two Hollander sisters. We got our birth certificates signed and notarized. Then we took a train to Göteborg. The Hungarian consulate required us to have a physical examination. No one with any illness would qualify for a visa.

"Don't offer the doctor any information about your past ailments," Iboya warned. "The less he knows, the better."

Iboya was relaxed during her exam, but never stopped talking to the doctor while he was checking me. "Piri is so healthy, you would never know she was in a concentration camp," she assured him. He kept writing down his findings on a form, hardly aware of Iboya's presence. It took over an hour, but in the end I passed.

Finally we had our pictures taken, and then our passports were ready. I looked just the way I felt—sad and wary. "Piri Davidowitz, 5 feet 2 inches, 103 pounds, oval face, straight nose, dark hair, brown eyes." It all looked official as I signed my name under the photograph.

The woman at the front desk shook our hands and congratulated us on passing all the requirements. "You can expect to hear from us within three to four months, at which time you'll have two months before sailing."

After we walked outside, Iboya gave a big sigh of relief. "God, you made it! Now you better take care that nothing happens to you within the next few months. I won't be able to relax till we're actually on that boat."

While in Göteborg, we were staying at Rulle's uncle's house. He had been a widower and recently married a Hungarian woman who was a survivor of the camps, like ourselves. She made us feel right at home and asked that we call her by her first name, Besi. Her children had perished in Auschwitz, she told us. "So God was good to me and now I have a second family. I even acquired a grandson. My husband's daughter can't have children. She and her husband have been married seven years. They have everything else, but God did not bless them with a child. Last spring, they adopted a little boy through a rabbi. Just wait till you see him. He is the most beautiful baby anybody has ever seen. Morris has carrot-colored hair, blue eyes, and white skin." Iboya and I looked at each other. "And he smiles all the time."

Just then her husband came in. "Why shouldn't he be happy? He knows that we are all his slaves. He drops a toy and six people jump to pick it up."

"You spoil him worse than any of us," said Besi.

The daughter and son-in-law arrived, followed by a nurse in a white uniform. She was maneuvering a stroller up the walk that looked more like a small car. Besi and her husband were already out the door. The nurse put a finger on her lips and signaled that the baby was asleep. She sat down on a garden bench and parked the stroller nearby so she could watch it. After a few moments of indecision, I could bear it no longer and walked out into the garden, trying to act nonchalant. I approached the stroller on tiptoe. The nurse's hand automatically reached for its handle and started it rocking. I gave her a friendly smile as I took a long look at the child. It was Dora's baby. The ringlets poking out of his cap were a deeper rust and thicker than the pinkish silky strands I remembered. He was also twice as big. But the china-white skin that looked too fair for a boy was his. I thought of what Dora had said when we commented on it—"He will freckle the first time he is exposed to the sun and never tan, just like his father." There were a few small dots on either cheek, or was I imagining them?

The nurse gave me a puzzled look. I answered it with another forced smile and whispered, "He is beautiful, just like Fru Galomb said." She smiled back in agreement. Iboya studied my face when I returned, but we did not get to speak until after Morris woke up and everyone was busy playing with him.

"Now, don't get carried away, Piri. Dora is not the only woman who ever had a redheaded baby," Iboya said, but I saw her turn pale when she looked at the baby as Besi carried him into the house.

"You don't think it's Jani?" I asked. "I suppose it is just a coincidence that they got him from a rabbi and that they were born the same time."

"Forget Jani, this is Morris. He belongs to the Galombs. They adore him and they can give him everything he will ever need. We saw a one-month-old infant; this child is over a year old. How could we recognize him? Get it out of your head, and don't stare at him!"

Morris was standing in the middle of the screened-in porch wearing a knitted short-pants outfit, looking just like a large doll. The family sat around in cushioned wicker chairs, each one offering him a bribe. Morris was finally persuaded by the jingling of the keys his grandfather was holding, and he took several unsure steps, collapsing onto his backside just short of reaching them. Everyone applauded, but Morris was frustrated and hit his chunky knees with his hands.

Grandpa picked him up and gave him the keys. "There, there."

"Oh, so you don't give in to him," said Besi, grinning.

In spite of the churnings inside me, I could hardly wait for Morris to notice me. He came in my direction on wobbly legs. His eyes never blinked but stared at my extended arm as I waved a red scarf toward him. We all held our breath as he proceeded up the six steps and snatched the scarf out of my hand. Then he toppled at my feet and looked up at me in satisfaction. I sat down on the rug alongside him. What ransom Dora would be willing to give, I thought, to be in my place at this moment.

When we left Göteborg and traveled on the train back to Rulle's family, I had a strong feeling that I would always remember Morris. On our arrival, Ulla informed me that Zigi had phoned in our absence and would be stopping in later that day. "Is Zigi your boyfriend?" she asked. "Has he visited you in Astorp? I can't imagine what he would be like on a date. Even when we were children, he was always so odd, we could never guess his thoughts. All the girls in high school tried to draw him out and invite him to socials, but he was like a hermit. Please," Ulla asked, "tell me about this man I grew up with and know nothing about."

I became as suspicious of her prying as she was curious. My suspicions were confirmed as soon as Zigi walked into the living room. By the time he gave Ulla a peck on the cheek, her whole face was flushed. After some polite conversation, Zigi insisted we hurry so as not to miss the Bing Crosby film he wanted to take me to.

When I confronted him with my observation about Ulla, he brushed it aside. "Our families were so close during our growing years that we are practically related."

After the movie, sitting in a coffeehouse, Zigi bought a newspaper from a carrier who shouted out the headline

PEACE TALKS IN THE MIDDLE EAST. Zigi immersed himself in the front page. I read over his tense shoulders: "Count Bernadotte was appointed mediator of Palestine by the United Nations." The article praised his cunning bargaining with the Germans, which saved thousands of prisoners during the war. It also spoke of his long devotion to the Swedish Red Cross and prophesied his bringing about peaceful negotiations between the Jews and the Arabs. The world was hoping for an Arab-Israeli armistice by the summer of 1948.

"Are you familiar with Bernadotte's work?" Zigi asked, looking up and folding the paper.

"Yes, I know a girl whose life he saved."

"Tell me about it."

"It happened during the winter of 1944. She was part of a transport that was abandoned near the Danish border without food or facilities. By the time her freight car was opened several days later by Bernadotte's group, only about a dozen of the hundred who had started were still breathing. She crawled out from under the corpses and was taken to a hospital in Denmark. She and I ended up in the same quarantine in Sweden." I finished with a shudder, remembering her speaking of the conditions in that cattle car.

"Yes, there were a few who were willing to take risks and get involved, but not enough," Zigi said.

"Do you think there will ever be peace in Palestine? My sister Etu's last letter was full of anticipation because the British were finally leaving, but I'm not sure if that will be an improvement."

Zigi smiled. "I believe that if anyone can accomplish a settlement among such hostile countries, it will be Bernadotte. I'm predicting shalom," he said, clinking his coffee cup to mine.

My mood lightened. Zigi also told me that his boat was

ready. "We have been testing her on short voyages and she sails like a dream. We'll soon be off into big waters."

"Crossing the Atlantic—it sounds so daring," I said. Zigi threw back his head and laughed. I reacted to his tremendous sex appeal with a start.

He must have read my mind. Turning serious, he asked, "Will you miss me, or are you fickle like all other women?" He looked disillusioned, as if his heart had been broken.

"Poor Zigi has been jilted by women," I jested, then felt sorry. "I bet many women adore you."

"Only my mother," he answered straight-faced.

He came to see me off the next day. The train was delayed at the station. I leaned out the window, and my hair came undone from its high pompadour and was blown across my face. Zigi's fingers brushed it aside, and he cupped my chin. We kissed, savoring the moments allotted us. Iboya looked on, confused. When I wrote to her later, I offered the only explanation I had. "There is something about parting at a railroad station that makes you anxious about the people who see you off."

Erik greeted me at the other end of my journey and I fell into his arms, overcome with guilt. I buried my face in his chest, afraid he might guess the reason for my unstable behavior.

I was back only a few days when Mama called me to the phone, saying, "You'll never guess who it is." I reached for the receiver.

"Piri, have you heard the news? Palestine has just been established as a Jewish state. After two thousand years, we have a homeland again!"

The voice was familiar, but I had to ask, "Who is calling, please?"

"Dr. Abrahamson. I just heard it on the radio, and I had to share it, so I thought of you."

"Thank you very much, I understand." I realized too late that I had replaced the receiver while Dr. Abrahamson was still talking. Mama was standing by, wondering about his calling me. I could not explain, so I turned on the radio. The announcement was repeated by a newsman, who reflected on the six million Jews killed, and on the rejoicing by Jews all over the world for the new state of Israel.

Papa brought home the newspaper and read it out loud to an excited Mama, busy with her dinner preparations. Dear Mama had a way of converting joy into festive meals, while Papa could only derive happiness by having it reflect from others. During his reading, he held a firm arm about my shoulder, giving me a side glance from time to time, to make sure that I was in full grasp of the article and its importance. It described the magnitude of the birth of a new state for a people with five thousand years of history behind them—a history of dispersement to all corners of the earth. As I listened, I wondered if we could now stop wandering. If so, would we become a people more nationalistic than religious? Papa finished his recitation while I helped Mama by setting the table.

Erik arrived to participate in the celebration. "Piri, I'm so happy for you and your sisters, congratulations. We must have a toast." He opened the bottle of wine he had brought and filled three glasses. "Skol, Piri, to Israel."

"And to Bernadotte, our good Samaritan," I said.

As I sipped the sweet red wine, I recalled the many goblets we had offered up at various family seders, declaring, "Next year in Jerusalem."

The following week there was a front-page article in the newspaper: THIRTEEN YOUNG ENGINEERS LOST IN THE ATLANTIC. SHIP WRECKED IN HEAVY STORMS. My eyes lingered in disbelief on one of the names listed—Sigurd Mattus. Making myself concentrate I read: "The Swedish Viking ship *Ormen Friske* was wrecked on its way from Mälaren to Le Havre with thirteen men aboard. A fisherman found a three-foot piece of the ship's stern on a sandbank off the west German coast . . ."

Iboya telephoned. "All of Jonkoping is in mourning; everybody is talking about it."

Ulla got on the phone. I could hardly distinguish the words between her sobs. I was numb, wishing I, too, could cry, but my eyes were dry.

My head throbbed. I took aspirin, Mama made me tea. Papa tiptoed around, watching my face. Erik was never more loving. He tried to give me hope. "They might still be found," he said. I felt guilty receiving so much sympathy, knowing that whatever Zigi and I had shared was without permanence, that I would overcome the tragedy without scars.

I called Iboya a few days later, hoping that she might have heard some shred of good news. Instead, she was anxious to tell me about a letter she had received from Etu. Something about her meeting Shafar, but I wasn't interested.

"I'll mail you the letter," she said. "Can you believe it, he is alive and married. I just can't get over it. Life is so strange . . ."

"Tell me about Zigi. Have you heard from his family?"

"Only that his mother is in a hospital with a nervous breakdown."

I remembered Zigi's words in the café in Jonkoping

when I had said, "I bet many women adore you." "Only my mother," he had answered. Tears finally washed over my face. I cried for Zigi's mother and for Zigi, and for all mothers who lose sons.

Iboya forwarded the letter from Etu. It seemed that as soon as the English left Israel, immigration opened up and all the people from Cyprus and other camps came pouring in. Etu and Geza were living on a kibbutz.

The communal life has many advantages, but we still long for our own apartment, no matter how small. I don't want to be governed by rules any longer, I just want to be on my own.

You two go on to America for now. This country needs settling in, and the constant harassment from the neighboring Arabs makes daily existence very tense.

Iboya, you will never guess whom I met last week. Your boyfriend Shafar Joska. There was a memorial service for the dead victims of Beregszász at a cemetery near Jerusalem. I traveled on buses all day to get there. Standing on a hill that overlooked the whole city, with the sound of Yizkor filling my ears, I was tapped on the shoulder. You can imagine my shock when I turned to see Shafar standing next to me, as if he had leaped out of one of the graves there. We went to the cafeteria at the bottom of the hill and talked over several cups of coffee. The world is both vast and small. We meet in Palestine, oceans and lands away from home, yet would you believe that he, too, had gone home to Beregszász at the end of the war and we missed each other?

It seems that after you were taken from the ghetto to Auschwitz, Shafar decided not to let them cart him away with his family and escaped that very night on a fire truck to the railroad station. From there, he purchased tickets on different trains, posing as a Christian, till he eventually reached Budapest. By doing odd jobs, he was able to obtain some ration coupons and stay alive. Dear Iboya, he told me how he had tried to persuade you to run away with him the night before you were taken. It was so noble of you to decline because you felt that your place was with Mother and the younger children. Just in case you ever had second thoughts about not joining Shafar, I really don't know if your fate would have been less traumatic if you had. As the political climate in Budapest worsened drastically, Shafar could no longer chance standing in employment lines, because the Germans made regular checks, forcing the men to undress and deporting any Jews they discovered to concentration camps. So Shafar hid in a cave outside the city until hunger made him register in the draft luring Jewish men out of hiding. Aside from the hunger, he was nagged by guilt for deserting his family in the ghetto. "I was born a Jew, I will die a Jew," he told himself when he signed up. Instead of the promised army with daily rations, he wound up in some distant forest, where he had to cut down a quota of timber every day in freezing winter conditions, for a payment of a bowl of thin soup. By midwinter, half the young men had starved and frozen to death. The other half, including Shafar, were hauled off to a concentration camp.

One night Shafar resorted to sleeping out in the open under a big tree because he did not have the energy to drag himself back into his barrack. Dysentery had robbed him of all strength. He was awakened by a rumbling of bombs. The tree he was under had been hit, and he was pinned down. He watched several inmates' bodies being thrown through the air. Shafar felt pain in his left hip and was afraid to examine the damage. Then he saw men rushing from the barracks, gathering up severed limbs, starting fires, cooking the flesh, and devouring it. He called on God to witness the event, while he struggled to free himself from the thick trunk of the fallen tree.

Bleeding from his hip wound, with fever racking his body and madness surrounding him, threatening his sanity, he dragged himself to the fence. He had observed that in the camp next to his some order was still maintained, and the prisoners were being served a bowl of soup at the end of their workday. He also noticed a pipe wedged under the wire fence to channel rainwater. Pretending to be washing himself, in case the guards spotted him, he managed to work his skeletal body through the pipe. The chaos created by the bombs kept him from being detected. Thus Shafar managed to hold death off for the last few weeks of his imprisonment.

By the time his camp was liberated, his hip wound was festering and he was unable to stand up. He got around by crawling on his stomach like a snail. He had to spend several months in a hospital till he had recovered sufficiently to travel home to look for his family and for you, dear Iboya. By then, Geza and I had left in despair for Palestine, so we just missed each other for the second time—first in Budapest and then in Beregszász. You would think the law of averages would have allowed us to meet in Cyprus. Yes, Iboya, we were both in Cyprus at the same time as well, but in different divisions. With such a huge number of people, even sisters and brothers were separated. Finally Shafar resigned himself to your having perished, and he married a woman from Romania. They already have a child. He had a hard time telling me about his marriage, as if he had betrayed you by not waiting longer, so I hurried to explain that you, too, had resigned yourself to his being lost, and that you are engaged (unofficially) to a young Swedish man. His face jerked and he offered no comment, just sat nodding his head. He has matured into an exceedingly handsome man. Then, as if there was nothing more to say, he excused himself. Coming back a few seconds later, twisting a cotton kibbutz hat in his strong hands, he said, "Please convey my wishes of happiness to Iboya the next time you write." We promised to keep in touch.

After finishing Etu's letter, I sat thinking of how long-range plans usually fall by the wayside. I had overheard Babi and Mother on occasion talking about the tragedies of life, when one of them would comment, "It is kind that we don't know our destiny." I forgave Iboya for not being able to think of anything but Shafar when I called to inquire about Zigi. I felt ashamed for my impatience with her on the telephone.

The next thing I heard from her was that she and Rulle had decided to get married before we sailed to America. Knowing Iboya, I was sure that learning about Shafar had had something to do with her decision. She needed a clear conscience before making a firm commitment.

Meanwhile, I was spending more time with Erik. The warmer months were very busy for him and I went along on many of his assignments, mostly weddings. I loved watching him work. He was so professional, arranging the bride and groom, and grouping the bridal party. I enjoyed seeing the respect all these people showed him; it made me feel important to be his date. They often made remarks like "Who will take the pictures when you two are married?" I no longer bothered to explain that I was going to America, because of comments like "What a shame."

On sunny weekends we would go to our favorite spot on the hill for picnics, or just to sit and watch the countryside. I would run from patch to patch of wild flowers, gathering them into a bright bouquet. Erik would spread his jacket on the soft grass and we would lie on our backs, looking up at the trees all bedecked with new leaves and blossoms. Through the umbrella of branches, we would watch the flawless blue sky with lazy white clouds screening out the glare of the sun.

One of these perfect days happened on my eighteenth birthday, June 10. Mama made a special dinner and invited Erik's parents. I had not seen much of them the last two months. Ever since my trip to America had been finalized, an awkwardness had developed between Fru

Olson and myself. Herr Olson was always polite when I was over, but I could sense a change in his attitude, too, an unspoken accusation—"You are hurting my son!" But this day they came with gifts and cheerful smiles. I was grateful to them, not only for making my birthday joyous, but for Erik's sake as well. It seemed to mean so much to him to get his parents' approval.

The standard gift for birthdays in Sweden is flowers. I had received several bouquets, the biggest from Nore and Greta. A single velvety red rose came without a card. I thought of Zigi; it was something he would have sent.

Erik was trying to save his gift till the next day, because he had planned to take me on a boat ride and wanted to present it to me while we were alone. But after our festive dinner, as I was unwrapping the toiletry case from the Olsons and the large valise from Mama and Papa, the mood suddenly grew heavy with evidence of my departure. Erik came to the rescue with a little speech: "Well, my gift to Piri is not as practical as yours, but I bet she will like it best of all." My hands shook as I was unwrapping the small package. I looked up into Erik's face; his eyes were urging me to go ahead and open it. The oblong box was lined with white satin and in it nestled a pink-gold watch. Erik wrapped it around my wrist and fastened the complicated clasp. I promised to cherish it always.

I brought my left wrist to my sleepy eyes, admiring the simple lines of my birthday present. The face, a coppperish pink to match the case, had a dome crystal. Under it, the small hand was on nine and the big one on four. I allowed myself one drawn-out stretch to reflect on last night. I saw Erik's radiant face and heard him whisper, "You must always remember me when you look at the watch. You see, it is really a selfish gift . . ." I jumped out of bed and hurried to be ready by ten, checking my new watch every five minutes.

The boat was large and white. We stood on the deck and surveyed the water, looking into its depth. We spied the shore through a pair of binoculars Erik had brought along and watched the birds circling in search of prey. We were partially conscious of voices and laughter in the background, but did not turn to look.

Erik's white cotton jacket rippled in the wind. I was careful about what I said so as not to spoil our "luxury voyage." The whole idea of taking a trip, just for the sake of pleasure, was such a thrilling novelty for me.

On the shoreline we walked hand in hand, bought food, and picnicked on a bank. We sailed back at dusk. The whole panorama took on a different aura in the evening light. The splashing waves looked dark and mysterious. The splendid sky of the afternoon was now dotted with sporadic stars, the moon curtained by moving gray clouds. Instead of finding the water and sky forboding, I felt they were romantic. Erik's strong arm encircling me felt protective and stable. I wished the voyage would last the night. But, as all good things end too soon, we were on land before we were ready for it.

As we walked to the car, Erik asked, "Was the boat ride all you had anticipated?"

"It could not have been more perfect if you had wrapped it in a box and tied it with ribbons." All of our held-back desires of the long day surfaced as soon as we were alone in the car. I always felt restrained in public. We made a conspicuous couple, Erik so tall and Nordic and I, in contrast, petite, with my dark hair now way below my shoulders. People often turned to look at us. Erik's reaction was to pull me closer, whereas I tended to draw away. But I did not draw away tonight. Since we had come back from Stockholm, so much had happened to keep us physically and mentally apart. I took a deep breath and blew it out.

"Tired?" Erik asked.

"No, just happy."

"Then come closer."

I did. We were both in the driver's seat. Erik put on the radio. American music filtered out in a husky male voice. Erik crooned along, "Although we are oceans apart, I can't make you open your heart, but I can dream, can't I?" I leaned on his shoulder with my face touching his neck, where I could listen to and feel the vibrations of his throat. I felt contentment and affection—or was it love?

A long time had passed. The stars were snuffed out by heavy clouds that left us in secluded darkness. We hardly noticed till the rain came down, hitting the roof of the car. Erik straightened up and attempted to stretch. The car did not have enough room for his long body. Turning the engine back on filled the car with the voice of a stranger reading the midnight news bulletin. I reached for the knob and lowered the sound, saying, "I'm not ready to be woken up." We drove home savoring our day.

14

The next day, I received a letter from Dora saying that she and Hershi had set the date for their wedding. "I'm so ecstatic, I had to share it with someone who could understand and appreciate the meaning of this event in my life. I think I'm beginning to believe in God."

I ran into the house to tell my good news to Mama. She stroked my hair with that gentle caution of hers. I could sense that she was thinking of Erik and me.

In almost every way, Mama was very practical and sensible. That night when Papa was fantasizing about my absence being temporary and that I would soon come back to my Swedish parents, Mama sobered him up. "Piri is emigrating to America to be with her family, Allan; be realistic. Don't burden her with pity for you."

Seeing a mournful expression on Papa's face, I edged into his rocking chair and sat across his lap the way he liked me to before he was conscious of my filling out. Papa could not deal with painful situations.

"*Rida, rida, ranka.*" He hummed the nursery rhyme, rocking us to and fro. "You won't forget your Swedish papa, will you, Piri?"

"No, Papa," I promised with conviction.

"You'll send me one of those pipes with a silver lid, like the one your grandfather had from his children in

America? You'll be a rich lady with lots of money to spend at your will. That is a country with houses as big as palaces, and everyone rides in automobiles. You will have to keep your balance and not let it turn your head. It is important to remember that the more simple the man, the more God keeps him in His favor." This was the first sermon I had heard from Papa since I had come to Astorp. It took great effort on his part. "Now go and fill up your papa's old pipe and come back to sit with me while I smoke." As I reached for the humidor, I caught a glimpse of Mama in the breakfront mirror. She stood in the kitchen, hand-whipping some cream in a heavy ceramic bowl cupped in her left arm, turning the whisk in fast circles. I saw teardrops on her pink cheeks. She was obviously listening to Papa. I did not invade her privacy, pretending not to see her image in the glass.

"Tamp it down good and tight, so it burns slowly," Papa instructed. I handed him the pipe and struck the large wooden match. He held out his free arm, inviting me to resume our rocking. "Now that I've taught you to pack a decent pipe, you'll be going off and leaving us."

"You want me to send you that pipe with the silver lid, don't you?"

"Yes. Be sure it's of briar, and while you're at it, you better send your mama a large sack of rice and some coffee." Papa puffed contentedly.

Mama came in with two dishes of strawberries that I had picked earlier, topped with mounds of whipped cream, her composure restored. "If anybody happened to come in, they would never believe this scene. Allan, Piri is past eighteen."

"I don't know how that changes anything," Papa offered stubbornly but hesitatingly.

I slipped off his lap and went to sit at the dining-room

table next to Mama. "Aren't you having any strawberries?" I asked, knowing that she had given us the entire bowl.

"They have too many little seeds and would upset my stomach." Not convinced, I tried to feed her some of mine, but she guided the spoon to my mouth. "You don't want your mama to get sick," she said, pretending to be stern, but her hand involuntarily reached for me.

Summer in Sweden is eagerly received but late in coming. I could hear Mama downstairs busy with her latest project, converting our living room into a summer parlor. She had taken down the heavy winter drapes and thrown them over the carpet post. Alfred Parson and I took turns beating out the accumulation of dust. Before storing the drapes away, I asked Mama if I could help her hang the summer curtains.

"No, I have to starch them first. You go and do some of your own chores," she said, straining to pull on the slightly damp floral cotton slipcovers. They seemed to have shrunk in washing, but Mama's determined hands stretched them till they fit the upholstered pieces. Zipping the sides, she straightened up, supporting her lower back with both hands.

I shook my head in concern. "If you get sick, Papa will be angry."

"I'll be slowing down," she promised, but she went on restlessly diluting starch in the washtub.

I went upstairs to sort out my clothes. Mama had asked me to give away my old clothes ever since my figure had filled out, but I couldn't part with them. I tried them on, looking in the stand-up mirror, then hung them back in the closet with their seams ripped. I reached for my diary, but instead of making an entry, I started reading at random. "I can't take this with me," I gasped out loud.

Since it was written in Hungarian, I was confident that nobody in Astorp could read it, so I put down everything —including my fantasies about Erik. If my aunt or uncle in America got hold of these confessions, there would be no doubt in their minds that they had a deranged child on their hands. My fingers gripped the scrawled pages and ripped them out of the wooden covers.

Looking at the scattered pages littering my room, I felt remorse, as if I had torn fragments out of my life. In a panic, I jumped off my bed and gathered them up, smoothing them out. I took a long look at the blue ink etching of an official-looking building on the front cover. I opened the diary and read the four-line inscription, in Adele's neat handwriting:

Everybody has theirs
Nobody is free
Heaven alone is free of sorrows

Don't mourn,
Triumph.
Adele

Suddenly I became aware of the quiet in the house. Mama's movements had stopped. I hid the crumpled pages of the diary behind the dust ruffle of my bed and walked slowly down the stairs to look for her. In the living room, light filtered in through the starched sheer curtains, picking up the muted green background of the slipcovers and giving Mama's face a soft, younger appearance. Her left hand rested in her lap; the right, extended, held an envelope. "It has come." Mama spoke the words without expression. I took the letter from her limp arm as I sat down next to her. Close up, I did not like what the suffused green light had done to her. Her silky white hair was robbed of its brilliance; her face, somber, was etched with lines of age. I felt anger toward an unknown official at the consulate.

"Let's not tell Papa, not till after supper," she whispered, as if he were in the room. Mama pushed herself up from the sofa, leaving the letter on my lap, and went to put away the ironing board and start supper.

I brought up the sausage and casserole from the cellar, set the table, put out a large chunk of cheese, and filled the basket with bread and crackers. When Papa came in, greeting us with a big smile, we were too preoccupied to stop and notice him. "Should I go out and come back in? What does a man have to do around here to be welcomed home?" I ran to the door, with arms open. "That is much better," said Papa, returning my hug. He walked to the stove and gave Mama a peck on her cheek. "I could smell the baked sausage as soon as I entered the yard. What an aroma! Will we eat right away, or can I read the papers first?"

"Read your papers," said Mama.

Seated at the dining-room table, I stole a look at Mama's face. Her blue eyes were framed in dark circles, with the familiar white blisters in the inner corners. I dreaded the night.

Mama prolonged her tidying of the kitchen, removing the burners, scrubbing the stove, wiping the doors of the cabinets. When she reached for the broom, I took it from her hands. "I'll sweep up. You go and sit down with Papa. You have not rested all day." She gave me a look of resignation and walked on past the living room and up the stairs.

Putting away the broom and dustpan, I checked in on Papa. He was in his rocking chair, puffing on his pipe as he turned pages. I took my letter from under the cloth of the hutch where I had hidden it and ran to my room. Closing the door, I reached for a pencil on my desk to pry open the envelope without tearing the document. It was just an ordinary white sheet of paper folded in three. "Miss Piri Davidowitz, Please be advised that you will be sailing on the *Gripsholm* on 22 October 1948." I reread the date and only skimmed the rest of the letter. Checking my calendar, I realized that I had over three months. I ran in to tell Mama, but I was too late. She was gripped by pain. The dark circles under her eyes had turned black. She cast me an apologetic glance.

"Should I call the doctor?" I asked.

"No, nobody, just sit by me."

"Oh, Mama, I have good news. I won't have to leave till the end of October." I dropped my head on her bosom.

"Maybe this one won't be so bad," she whispered into my ear. I prayed in silence. "When in October?"

"The twenty-second. We'll have the whole summer together."

Mama managed a smile. I felt her body stiffen and then jerk under me. She grimaced and her arms reached for the sides of the bed.

The attack lasted several minutes. I went to the bathroom and prepared a cool towel. Some of the color had returned to her face. I placed the damp cloth around her forehead and sat down alongside her. We waited together for the next seizure. When I left her for a moment to freshen the towel, Mama screamed out in a new spasm of pain. Papa came running up, two steps at a time. Mama grabbed for his outstretched arms and squeezed till her knuckles turned white. I watched, holding my breath, till her long fingers relaxed.

"I knew you would have an attack when I saw you start with that heavy work downstairs," Papa scolded. He always needed an excuse, something to blame. He could not accept the fact that Mama had a sack of kidney stones that would continue to act up from time to time unless they consented to an operation. Papa sat, worn out by the episode, almost as if he had gone through it himself. I felt like getting a second towel for him.

"Go downstairs and Piri will call you when it comes again," Mama pleaded, leaning back on her pillow with her eyes shut.

He went to the kitchen but came right back with a cold drink. "Maybe it will help to wash it out."

Mama sat up and drank the water. They had a regular routine.

The spasms continued for hours. Mama kept moaning and thrashing like a woman in labor. It was after midnight by the time she passed two small stones. I heard them clank in the pan like pebbles. Exhausted, Mama crawled back to bed, giving herself to sleep.

I woke late the next morning. Reaching for my gold watch on the night table, I remembered last night's dream. There were two somber faces on one body—one of them was Mother's and the other one Mama's. My throat tightened in sorrow for both of them. Rushing downstairs without bothering to put on my robe, I found Mama fully dressed by the stove. She was pouring batter onto a sizzling griddle. It spread thin as paper. I walked on tiptoe and hugged her from the back. It was an uncommon gesture. Mama turned around and hugged me for all the times she had wanted to but hadn't. I held still, submitting with lingering pleasure. It was finally the smell of burning batter that separated us. With moist eyes and giggles, we went to work cleaning up the mess. For the rest of the day, we acted like embarrassed lovers whenever we happened to look at each other.

I once overheard Mama say to Papa, "I can't force myself on her; I'm not her real mother. She might resent it." I thought of how natural it was back in our house for all the girls to hug or snuggle up in bed. Mother's hugs, though, had to be earned by approval or in sympathy. Her reserve, I suspected, came from Babi's warning: "You're spoiling those girls, raising them without responsibilities or discipline." Compared to the hardworking farm children in Komjaty, I guess we were fancy free, but not compared to our city peers. As for my little brother, Sandor, there was no limit on affection when he was an infant. Father, Mother, and we girls never stopped touching him. I often got jealous, since I was the youngest before he came along. Being the fifth girl was not quite the same as being the first boy. As Sandor got a little older, we were held back by both Mother and Father from showing our love so exuberantly. Thinking now about all the restraints on affection I had had, I decided it was a big waste of time.

After breakfast I tried to call Erik to tell him about the letter. I took the receiver off and held it until I lost the dial tone.

Mama was watching. "You have to tell him, before he finds out about it from somebody else."

"How could he?"

"You know how news travels in Astorp," Mama said.

"But nobody knows."

"I told Papa, I knew you couldn't. They might run into each other."

"I'm going to the studio," I said, halfway out the door. It was a beautiful late morning. Some of the neighbors were in their yards. I called to them, "*God dag!*" One of Mama's friends stopped hanging her wash and walked to the fence to talk with me. I did not want to be rude, but I was in the middle of silently rehearsing how I would tell Erik about my date of departure. "Yes, it is a heavenly day, Fru Peterson, but I'm on an urgent errand—

I hope you will forgive me," I called back to her, and hurried on. I could see her surprise; usually I was more than willing to socialize.

No matter how I phrased the words, the meaning remained the same—"I'm leaving you." I wished that I could just send Erik a telegram. I felt disappointed in myself for being such a coward. The closer I got to the studio, the slower I walked. I tried out excuses why this was not a good time to tell him: "Why not tonight, when we can be alone and he is finished with work for the day?" It was only having to face Mama that finally made me approach the studio.

Erik was standing in the doorway, talking to a customer, but I did not see them. My head was down, still rehearsing. I almost bumped into them, reaching for the door. The man bowed in apology and greeting, and walked away. Erik pulled me in. He studied my face a moment, then saved me my speech. "You heard from the consulate," he blurted out.

"I got the letter yesterday, but Mama was sick, and . . . I don't have to leave till the twenty-second of October."

Erik walked over to the calendar. "When exactly will you have to leave Astorp?"

"I don't know yet, I'll have to speak with my sister."

"I want to take my vacation the last two weeks you're here." Erik took my hand again and led me into the inner office. He stood with his back against the door and pulled me toward him. By the time he kissed me, I felt like gelatin. I knew he was aware of my emotional state and I was no longer embarrassed by it. I would not have wanted Erik to think that our relationship meant less to me than it did to him.

Iboya called that evening. She was as stirred up about our departure as I, and had just as many plans for the short time allotted us. She and Rulle had already made arrangements with a judge who was a family friend to marry them. "Can you be here by the beginning of September?" she asked me. "We want to set a definite date. Also, you and I will have to go to Göteborg a few days early, before we leave." As I was listening, I saw the apportioned time dwindle down to six weeks.

Mama, as usual, could read my face. After I hung up and related my conversation with Iboya, hers took on the same expression. "I made so many plans for us. I called Anders and they invited us to come to their summer house—Papa has a whole month off. We can't disappoint him."

Up in my room, I tried to sort out my thoughts, but my pent-up crying surfaced and gave me a headache. I reached for my diary but remembered that I had destroyed most of the pages. For a moment I considered making an entry in Swedish, but then felt it was futile.

Papa came knocking on my door. It was so unnatural to see him melancholy. He walked to my window and looked out onto the street. "How long have you been here, Piri?"

"Fourteen months, Papa."

"Well, it is not the length of time but what happens, and what we make of it, that counts." I got off my bed, and he turned to face me. I felt such comfort in his arms that I found myself smiling up at him. By the time we joined Mama in the kitchen, we were both making jokes.

15

Erik joined us on our trip to Anders's summer house for the last two weeks of August. His having a car was a big help. We traveled mostly on country roads that sometimes passed through towns.

As we drove down the dirt driveway of a lakeside cottage, Anders and Britta came out to meet us. While Mama hugged her granddaughters Birgitta and Ingegerd, the men shook hands. Then Anders gave me an odd, questioning look. I removed my sunglasses. "Is this really my little sister?" he gasped.

"I don't like the way you look at her," Papa said. "You better watch out for Erik."

We had not seen each other since Christmas. I was flattered. I considered Anders an authority on looks because he was a very handsome man and because he had such a beautiful wife. I was sure he could have chosen anyone he pleased.

In Astorp people seldom made a comment on looks. It did not seem to be an important attribute to them. But I remembered from my childhood in Hungary that beauty for women was critical. I heard people refer to my mother as "the pretty woman down the street." A girl could hardly hope to get a husband if she was ugly.

It took a lot of juggling to get us settled in the small

country house. There were only two bedrooms. Anders and his wife slept in the master bedroom; the girls moved into the sunroom and gave their room to Mama and Papa. I was to sleep on the couch in the parlor and Erik was put up in the gatehouse. "This way, you won't disturb anyone if you come in late, or early in the morning," Anders commented with a knowing glance at Erik. I'm sure I turned red.

The weather was typical of Swedish summers, the sun barely strong enough to warm the water in the lake above 21 degrees centigrade. But Erik and I swam and splashed just the same. Then we would lie in the sun, taking advantage of its limited rays. We took many long walks. Our holiday had a touch of bittersweet, but we did not let it spoil our visit with the family and our last days together. We took rides and found a spot on a hill similar to our favorite one in Astorp. It was secluded; our only company was an occasional rabbit or woodchuck. Once, a four-legged red-furred intruder wearing spectacles dared to loiter so close that I held on to Erik in fright. Evidently we were as much a novelty to him as he was to us. He stood staring at us for several minutes. It was finally Erik's amused laughter from watching me inch on top of him that startled our uninvited guest away. Erik never ceased to be astonished when something alarmed me.

One afternoon we rented a rowboat on a larger lake nearby and rowed and drifted the hours away. When Erik took off his shirt, I was surprised to see how powerful his arms were. He handled the oars and maneuvered the boat with easy grace. A true Viking, I thought admiringly.

"Where did you learn to steer a boat?" I asked him.

"Oh, when I was a kid. Then while I was in high school I competed on a team."

As soon as he said "high school," I pictured Ingrid, with her long legs, wearing a seductive bathing suit in my place. I was dying to ask if he had taken her rowing, but I controlled myself, not wanting to argue.

In the back of my mind, I was very much aware of time running out, but I tried not to think about it, to the point that I lost track of what day of the week it was. When Mama said, "Since tomorrow is our last day here, Papa would like to take us all out for dinner," I had a jolt; I was sure that we still had two days left.

Silence dominated our ride back home. I sat next to Erik, who was suntanned and rested. While he concentrated on the road, from time to time he would reach for my hand. Papa dozed, and Mama remarked, "I'll be glad to sleep in my own bed tonight."

When we got home, there was a note stuck in our door from Lisa across the street. "Hasse and I would like to invite you and Erik over for an evening before you leave. Would Friday be convenient?" Mama was more surprised than I that I had been invited to the Andersons' house. "Well, I guess you are no longer a threat," she said, "since you'll be leaving." Erik and I had not seen much of Lisa and Hasse lately, preferring to be by ourselves.

Like Gullan's parents, Lisa's were not visible at her party. All the official members of Charlie's group were present. They tried hard to be cheerful. Many jokes were told, to unspontaneous laughter. But one thing was certain and sincere—their respect for Erik. In spite of his involvement with an *utlänninger*, an outsider, his standing was unblemished.

I overheard Britt complimenting him: "You should spend more time in the sun, it really does something for you. I know this place near . . ." I could not hear the rest of the sentence because of the other voices in the room. Britt was married, with a child, her husband away in the army. Before Erik and I used to go out together, I would babysit for her two-year-old daughter, Solig (Sunny). Never has there been a more fitting name, yet Britt would get very cross with her. Mama said she resented the child for tying her down; she was only twenty-one.

I watched the guests I had known for the last year and was more aware than ever that I had never really been a part of this circle. They stood in clusters holding drinks, laughing. The awkwardness about the reason for the party was washed down by spirits. Involved as they were in each other, I could have been on a boat out at sea. I thought of what Dr. Abrahamson had said: "Erik belongs with his own kind."

Erik came and squatted by my chair, startling me. "Don't sit here alone, come join the party or Lisa will think us ungrateful."

I tried to collect myself. "I'll come in a minute; you go back and talk to Britt."

Erik did not move. "You are in one of your black moods; you know she doesn't mean anything to me."

"They all mean a lot to you, a lot more than I. You are friends, with your whole lives in common; I'm an outsider." I felt hurt, my voice sounded hostile and accusing. I wished Erik would leave me alone and let me wallow in my sulking. He glanced around to see if we had been observed. Hardly. The others never seemed to run out of conversation.

"They lead such a boring existence and pretend that it is interesting," I said with an air of superiority.

"Would you like to go?" Erik asked, just a bit annoyed at my behavior.

I got out of my chair and moved toward the cluster with Britt. "How is Solig?" I asked.

"She still speaks of you," Britt answered. "You were her favorite sitter, and now you'll be leaving. She would probably cry if I told her."

"Please give her a kiss for me, I will remember her." I walked over to Lisa. "Thank you so much for having this farewell party for me . . ."

Lisa cut me off in mid-sentence. "You can't go yet, we have a gift for you."

Hasse came rushing over. "It is early, I never even got a chance to speak with you."

"I have so much to do, I have not packed."

"It is only 10:00 P.M., can't you stay another hour?" Hasse looked to Erik for an answer, but Erik was noncommittal.

"I guess I could stay a bit longer," I said.

Hasse turned back to me. "When do you actually sail?"

"The twenty-second."

"How I wish that you could take me along in your trunk."

"And what would Gullan have to say about that?" I heard myself ask in a cunning voice.

"Why tell her," retorted Hasse.

I looked back and saw Erik with an "I can't believe it" expression on his face. I tried to imitate Britt in my flirting with Hasse, enjoying Erik's shock and Hasse's surprise.

Hasse went to refill my punch cup, which was still half full, and got himself another beer. He was edging his face down to mine and decided to try out his high-school German—the words "*Ich liebe dich, Fräulein,*" I love you, miss, came out punctuated with whiffs of beer. I was not drunk, but the sound of the German words and the smell of beer had a sobering effect on me. I saw Hasse, deceitful, and myself, ugly, full of revenge, and a frightened little girl about to be loaded onto a train to Auschwitz.

A crude man not much older than Hasse, speaking German and reeking of sausage and beer, held the back of her neck in an iron grip while he searched her private parts and laughed at her shame. Shaken, I walked away, put down my glass, and headed for the door.

Lisa stopped me. "It is not yet eleven o'clock."

"Lisa, I really must go home."

"Then wait a moment." She returned with a box. I unwrapped a beautiful leather picture album while everyone gathered around me. "Open it," Lisa urged. On the first page was a photo of Charlie with signatures surrounding it. My face burned with humiliation for my unkind thoughts and behavior. How could I condemn them for being insensitive when they were so generous and thoughtful? I was preoccupied with self-pity. What did I expect from these people, anyway? I put the album back in the box and placed it on a table.

I heard my husky voice reciting an impromptu speech. "I appreciate your taking the trouble for me, with this party, the beautiful album, and, most important, your friendship during my stay in Astorp. It made me feel good to belong to a group. Thank you." That was as much as I could manage before the tears welled up in my eyes. I was surprised to see that I had company. Several of my Swedish friends were sniffling as they bade me farewell and bon voyage.

The next day, when Erik called to find out if I had had a good night's sleep and if I felt better, I remembered my flirting with Hasse and was ashamed. Then I pictured Erik talking intimately with Britt. Just thinking about it, I was consumed with rage. "What about you, did you dream about Britt?"

"Piri, let's forget last night, it was just a party. Nobody takes any of it seriously." Again I was reminded of my taking things too seriously. I had been aware of it many times before, but didn't like Erik's bringing it to my attention.

"Oh, I'm glad that I'm leaving here, I would never fit in. You laugh at things I think serious, and cry at what I think unworthy trivia. How could we ever understand each other?"

After a pause, Erik asked, "Can I come over?"

"Yes, come over." I sobbed after replacing the receiver.

Mama came to soothe me. "Piri, why don't you take one of those pills Dr. Abrahamson gave you."

I was more or less composed by the time Erik arrived. We went for a ride and stopped at our spot on the hill. We did not sit on the grass, just stood and looked down at Astorp. It was not a very impressive place, with its ordinary rows of houses, so why was I so moved? Erik led me on a walk. The bit of forest was dry, we had not had much rain in July or August. I stopped to pick a lone purplish flower from its withered stem and pulled it through the top buttonhole in Erik's white shirt. Looking into my face with sad eyes, he asked, "You don't really think that our differences can't be bridged? I'm so sorry about last night, I wish I could undo the injury. We should have spent it by ourselves and not squandered it away. They meant well, of course, but we have so little time. Is there anything you would like to do tonight?"

"Some people will stop in to say goodbye, Mama told me. Greta, Nore, and Papa will see me off tomorrow; Mama doesn't want to come to the train."

"I don't want to come either, but I'll be there." We closed the short distance between us. "*Jag älskar dig,*" whispered Erik, three short powerful words that reached deep inside me. I wondered why I had yearned so long to hear them. Wasn't I convinced of his love before, or was I that insecure or so incurably romantic?

I was not sure, only that I felt an overflowing joy that made me whisper back, "*Jag älskar dig.*"

Later that evening we went dancing with Greta and Nore. Nore, having managed a weekend pass so he could see me off, had made a last attempt "to talk some sense into me," as he called it. "You know, it still is not too late to change your mind. It is done all the time. People get sick or there is a death in the family. They just notify the next person on the waiting list that they can take your place."

Nore insisted I have a mixed alcoholic drink. I had never tried anything stronger than wine or spiked punch before. It tasted sweet and fruity. After the second one I could hardly feel my legs. Before long, Greta started her usual clinging to Nore, making it uncomfortably obvious that she would rather leave and be alone with her fiancé. This time, Nore let himself be persuaded without much coaxing. While he paid the bill, Erik went to get Charlie.

When we dropped them off at Greta's house, Nore said to Erik, "Why don't you sleep over in my bed, rather than having to come back in the morning? We'll meet you at the station around 10:00 A.M."

Erik acknowledged the invitation with a wave of his hand. The house was quiet. My large suitcase was in the foyer; Papa must have brought it down. We walked around it, avoiding it like an enemy. Lying down on the living-room sofa, I felt the room spin. I undid a few buttons on Erik's shirt and rested my head on his chest. He felt warm and very still.

An internal disturbance awakened me—an awareness of the passing of time. Somewhere an appointment had to be kept; I was scared that I had missed it. When I opened my eyes, reality hit me—my appointment was with a train, and I was sleeping with Erik. Our last night. I was anxious to check the hour, but I did not want to wake Erik by disentangling myself from him. I waited until he moved of his own accord.

It was 8:00 A.M. Erik's clothes were rumpled as he staggered to the bathroom to wash up. I made a dash upstairs to change my dress.

Mama came into my room. "Is Erik still here?"

"Yes, we fell asleep on the sofa."

"Do you need help with anything before I go down to prepare breakfast?"

"No, I'm all packed, thank you. I only need to wash and change my clothes." I put on my new green suit, made just for this occasion. It had been hanging in my closet since early spring. I would look at it from time to time, thinking, Someday. It was like thinking of someday having to die.

The dressmaker assured me that my suit was the latest fashion in the United States. It had a straight skirt with a side zipper and a back slit, and it practically reached my ankles. "No more than ten inches from the floor; I consulted the Vogue pattern book," the seamstress insisted. Mama and I persuaded her to raise it to twelve inches.

Checking in the mirror as I was getting ready, I looked as if I had put on a tall person's clothes. The form-fitting jacket was supposed to cinch the waist and flare out in a cape effect, encircling the hip. It just hung loose, doing neither. Mama took one look at me and declared, "You must have lost several kilos since that outfit was made. You better start eating in Jonkoping and during your ten-day voyage, or you won't look so stylish when you arrive, in spite of our dressmaker's efforts."

I caught Erik's eyes traveling down to my hemline. They filled with mirth, in spite of himself. That did it! I ran up to my room, got my wrinkled dress, came down, pulled out the ironing board, and proceeded to press the heavy iron into the stubborn creases. Mama watched for a few seconds in silence, then said quietly, "Why not take out another dress?"

"I don't want to open my suitcase, I'll never be able to close it again."

She reached for the iron. "Here, I'll do it, you go have breakfast."

At the table, Papa picked up his pipe. "Well, I might as well walk down to the station and make sure the trains are running." His eggs and sausage were hardly touched.

"I'm sorry, Papa, please don't go, it is only nine o'clock. I promise to be good."

"I'm just going to get the paper and come right back." Erik and I were left alone in the kitchen. The clock ticked louder than I had ever heard it before. I sat down next to him; he gave me an absentminded smile.

"Have something to eat, you don't want to travel on an empty stomach," Mama called from the living room.

I was observing Erik while I sipped my coffee. His face was covered with a shadow of stubble and there were dark circles under his eyes. I had an urge to take care of him. Mama brought in my dress and I went up to change.

Papa returned with the newspaper. I ate breakfast, finished some last-minute packing, and noticed that Erik had shaved. Mama packed me lunch for the train and then Papa said, "It's 9:30, we should be getting started." I stared at the noisy clock in anger and realized that an hour and a half had gone by and I had not thought of anything to say. Erik picked up the large suitcase, Papa held the old satchel I came with, and Mama stood nervously waiting for me to say goodbye.

Nothing came, not words or action. In a stupor, I fumbled to embrace Mama. "I want to say so much,

Mama, you have been almost like my own . . . Take care, don't be sick." I kissed her blindly. I could not take a last look.

Papa seemed lonely in the back seat. "Was she all right?" I nodded my head to assure him. "You must write to her. She will be looking for a letter."

Nore and Greta were waiting at the station with flowers. They seemed as anxious as if they were leaving. Greta was looking at Erik in pity. She cast me a look of "Oh, how could you?" We all took turns peering up and down the tracks. Papa was talking with a trainman. "America!" he said with awe. I heard a rumble in the distance. Nore said something to Erik, then he came over to say goodbye. His grip was strong, almost binding.

"Don't wait too long to make up your mind, he might not be here. You are a damn little fool" were my Swedish brother's parting words. Greta was crying.

Papa looked forlorn but determined to be brave. "Maybe it's meant to be, but it's hard just the same." After freeing himself from me, he walked over to the trainman and took the flag out of his hand. The train came into sight. I reached for Erik in alarm. We were still holding on, unable to let go, when Papa finally held up the flag to wave the train on.

A woman dabbing at her eyes with a handkerchief in sympathy called in a motherly tone of voice, "Come, sit next to me."

I was not aware that I was the only passenger boarding the 10:08 train from Astorp until I looked back and realized that the people on the platform were all waving to me. It looked desolate and eerie—Papa holding up the faded red flag, Erik just ahead of him, extending an arm that did not wave, Greta sobbing on Nore's stiff shoulder. The woman next to me tried to cheer me up. "Trains that take you away also bring you back."

The trains I had traveled on had not made many return trips in my past. They seemed to have gone only one way—away from my home and the people who mattered most to me. I had always been an optimist, but I was starting to believe that everything was transitory. I made a vow that in the future I would not hold back my affection from people I cared about. I had never stopped regretting my failure to use those final hours in the freight car to tell Mother how very much I loved her.

Iboya and Rulle greeted me at the station with the news that they were already married. "The judge called to tell us that he was leaving on his vacation," Iboya said, "and we had to make a quick decision. You did not miss much, we just went to his study. Rulle's mother is having some family and close friends to the house for dinner this evening."

"When I join you in America, we'll have a religious ceremony," Rulle rushed to add, seeing my disappointment.

There was the usual gathering of guests in the Slobodkins' salon. They all knew me by now as the little sister with the Skane accent. For their entertainment I enriched it more than need be.

The conversation was mostly politics pertaining to Israel. "We were not allowed to enjoy the declaration of a Jewish state for even one day. Those bloodthirsty Arabs started fighting while we were still listening to our radios about the armistice," one matron commented. "So disheartening for Bernadotte," said another. "He is a true count and a good friend of the Jews." The men were discussing the role of the United Nations in controlling the Arab aggression. "Bernadotte can only make proposals. The UN has to set the terms and enforce them."

Listening to them talk, I was most aware of their personal involvement with Israel—they, too, were dedicated Swedes, like the people of Astorp, but they spoke with pride of the new breed of Jews coming out of the Second World War. I thought of David and tried to picture him in one of the paratroopers' uniforms that I had seen in the newspaper.

Iboya came over to where I stood and took my hand. "I want you to meet some of Rulle's friends." She introduced me to a group of people standing in the hallway.

"So you are the one who is responsible for taking them to America," said a young man I recognized from our dances. He obviously did not recall meeting me.

Slightly irritated for not having made an impression on him, I countered, "No, I would really rather go to Israel."

I got just the reaction I was hoping for. He mumbled in confusion, "But I thought . . . why Israel?"

"To ease my conscience. Here we are discussing its fate as if we really cared, but without taking the least bit of risk." I was not lying about my conscience. Ever since the halutz had come to speak to us at school, I had felt guilty about not participating in the Zionist movement. In Astorp, when I was being congratulated on the establishment of Israel, it made me feel like a hypocrite and traitor. Now it all surfaced into rebellion against these innocent Swedish Jews.

After the guests left, I had a talk with Iboya. "You don't have to go to America on my account and leave Rulle. You needn't be a martyr for the second time. You gave up running away with Shafar from the ghetto because you wanted to be of help to Mother, but there's no crisis now."

Iboya's face became flushed with anger. "Listen, Piri, you have been living by a different set of rules in Astorp."

"You mean with people of a different religion," I remarked.

"I did not say better or worse, just different. It might not be all a religious difference, either; it could be part cultural. In any case, they don't have a history of five thousand years of persecution. It is written in the Bible that we must not reap our fields bare during harvest but always leave some on the stalks and branches for the poor. In other words, don't be selfish."

"Have you been reading the Bible lately?"

"No, I just didn't play hooky from Sunday school as often as you did." Iboya grew reflective, then added, "Besides, Mother entrusted me with looking after you, and I won't let her down." She saw the amazement on my face and explained, "Well, not really with words, but with her eyes as we were being separated. I know she was asking me to take care of you. I want her to be proud of me."

I let the remainder of my time in Jonkoping slip away. A good part of it I spent with Ulla; I visited the Hollander sisters, asked Hajnal to let me read her letter from Beregszász. When I reread the part about my little brother and his friend, it made me cry to know that someone would remember him. I copied the address and considered writing to Tomas, but didn't. What could I say to console him—"Dear Tomas, you have to face the harsh realities of life. He is never coming back"?

Many afternoons I walked to the phone booth around the corner from the Slobodkins, working myself up to call Erik. When the operator would ask, "Yes, what number would you like?" I would lose my nerve and hang up quickly.

Iboya, Rulle, and I were ready to go to the cinema one evening when the phone rang. Rulle picked it up. "Are you sure? When? Do they know who did it?" We turned toward Rulle questioningly. "Bernadotte has been shot." Aghast, we waited till he replaced the receiver. "It was Sara. She just heard on the radio—they interrupted that health program she always listens to."

"Is he dead?" Ulla dared to ask.

"Yes."

"It must have been a barbaric Arab," Sonya offered as the only acceptable explanation of such a cruel act.

Rulle was slow in answering. "All they know so far is that he was shot in the Israeli-held sector of Jerusalem."

We turned to Fru Slobodkin, who looked the portrait of an Old World matriarch. She said simply, "I hope we won't have to carry the guilt of this deed."

When we stood by the ocean liner with the name *Gripsholm* in large letters on its side, I watched Iboya and Rulle say goodbye and could hardly believe that I had been away from Erik for more than a month. As a matter of fact, as soon as I was back with Iboya and Rulle's family, Astorp seemed to become almost unimportant, like a vacation spot or a summer camp. The focus was on the future; I was the kid sister who had some maturing to do. "The family was kind, remarkable, to take in and care so much about a Jewish child; they are to be commended," I heard Mrs. Slobodkin repeatedly telling her friends about the Rantzows. As to my romantic involvement with Erik, Rulle's sisters listened with curiosity but without giving it any serious thought. Just like their mother, they considered the people in Astorp to be of a different stock, and my emotions only an infatuation. Amusing, like my Skane accent. Iboya, noticeably uncomfortable to hear about Erik, discouraged my discussing him with her, making him become my private reflection.

Aboard the *Gripsholm*, people were milling around in a frenzy of excitement. Every passenger had someone to see them off. They attempted to call and shout to one another across the distance separating them. The well-wishers on the shore were growing small and remote. Soon the sound of the ship's horn drowned out the voices. I waved to everyone and no one in particular. Another stage of my life was in the past.

Iboya and I could hardly find our way to our third-class passenger cabin through the maze of corridors. We were seasick. There were two double berths in the cabin. The other two women passengers tried to help by pointing out the seasickness bags and giving other useful hints. I climbed into my upper berth clutching the bag and missed five meal calls. The ship's doctor finally made us go up on deck for some sea air toward the end of the second day.

A young man by the name of Fritz helped me into a deck chair. "What you two need is a beer; it will make you feel better." Iboya refused, but I decided to try it. I could not feel worse, I reasoned. He brought me a frothy glass of black beer. It washed down smooth and settled my queasy stomach. I was grateful.

At dinner, Iboya and I found ourselves in the large dining room for third-class passengers. We were ushered to a table with other refugees emigrating to America. The waiter asked, "Did you two ladies just board?" Everyone laughed. We did not think it funny.

The first course was a sectioned grapefruit half. Not having seen one before, I sat looking and poking at it. One woman, whom we had met before in Göteborg, said, "It is bitter, don't eat it." I ate mine and two others; the flavor, I thought, resembled beer, which was also slightly bitter. I realized how hungry I was. During the many courses of food, I noticed that all the passengers except for Iboya and me were dressed up. I felt stale in my gray slacks and yellow sweater.

The next morning I made an effort to wash and change my clothes. Fresh air was the key to our recovery. I persuaded Iboya to join me on deck. She looked pale and forlorn, from seasickness and missing Rulle. I turned down an invitation from Fritz to go up to his lounge for a beer, so he brought some to our chairs. Iboya nursed hers like medicine till it went flat. Crowds and commotion were something she had not felt comfortable with since the camps.

I continued to have a beer with Fritz each day of our voyage. He was a law student at Harvard returning from a summer holiday with his family in Norway. He spoke to us in German; Iboya was suspicious of his impeccable accent. "I bet he comes from a German background," she said. I did not question his heritage, but accepted his friendship.

Ten days in the middle of the ocean is a long time. I read *Robinson Crusoe* in Swedish, wrote letters to my Swedish parents and Erik, and to Elu in Israel. I also filled the remaining pages of my diary with entries about our voyage. I marveled that so many days of sailing could go by without our catching a glimpse of land or even a bird—man seemed insignificant in the vast universe. On the last day, standing at the railing near the bow, I got into a discussion about it with Fritz. "I strongly disagree with you," he told me. "The reason I'm taking up law is to defend the rights of individuals. Every man is important; just one man alone can change the course of history for the whole world. Like Hitler, for instance. If it was not for him, there would not have been a Second World War, and you would not be here today searching for a new life."

"I would hate to take the blame away from him for

causing the war and the slaughter of eleven million," I said, "but he did not accomplish it single-handedly. He had many helpers."

"No, it was Hitler with his sick brain who masterminded this chapter of history. That is how it must be written. The other people's involvement was just a chain reaction. They were forced into it."

"You mean that, as a lawyer, you would plead the accomplices' innocence?"

"As I said, they were drawn into it by the climate of life that Hitler created. He set up the laws and made it dangerous not to cooperate. The men he drafted into the army were not killers. They were upstanding citizens with honorable professions, churchgoers with families, just like my father . . ."

Fritz's voice faltered; his face quivered. After a pause he declared, "I know for certain that my father was innocent! He died defending his country." Suddenly my nausea returned—coming to terms with the past was not yet over, and never would be. I would have to live with the Fritzes of the world—even try to understand their guilt, understand them, in hopes of making a better world.

I looked over to Iboya's chair a few feet away, knowing that the awakening would be harder for her.

"Piri, would you come up to the lounge in my class to have a farewell beer with me?" Fritz asked in an uncertain voice.

"Yes."

I mounted the stairs. Looking back just for a second, I saw a dark void spotted with yellow lights high in the watchtowers, and I heard Misha's voice—"Don't linger." I shuddered. Iboya's eyes followed us up the stairs full of question and concern. I kept climbing.